Crossroads

STORIES AT THE INTERSECTIONS

TED BOWMAN

D1473142

Interprovincial Board of Communication
Moravian Church in North America

Table of Contents

Foreword

When learning to drive, my parents urged me to be especially alert when driving through intersections. "Slow down, look both ways, and be alert" were advisory words I heard often before and after I began to drive. Little did I know then that my parents were giving me a life lesson, not just driver advice. As I have aged, I have become convinced that it is in life's crossroads — life and death, sickness and health, youth to aging, grief and hope, caregiver to care-receiver, school to work, belief and doubt, or from innocence to loss of innocence — that one needs to slow down, look both ways, and be alert.

The pieces in this book reflect my faith and my belief that it is in the intersections of life that God can be known most profoundly, sometimes through other voices or example, sometimes by silence and perceived inaction, and often through the continuity of creation. I also firmly believe God is still speaking! My challenge is having ears to hear, eyes to see, and the willingness to face my self, my relationships, and God. Discernment, in my experience, is no easy task. Writing forces me to pay attention. In some small way, I hope my stories and poems will encourage your own reflections. I'm reminded of Frederick Buechner's insight from an early memoir:

My story is important not because it is mine, God knows, but because if I tell it anything like right, the chances are you will recognize that in many ways it is also yours. Maybe nothing is more important than that we keep track, you and I, of these stories of who we are and where we have come from and the people we have met along the way…

As one of my grandchildren told me once, "Grampy, stories work!" I believe he was right!

Some Comments About the Format and Your Choices For Reading This Book

The pages that follow contain stories, poems, and reflections I have written. Some have been published; others have been for personal reflection or for sharing only within the family until now. Permission has been requested and given by those family members whose lives overlapped with mine. Permission, however, does not imply agreement. The stories of my family and friends, should they write or tell their versions, will be different than the words found here. Novelist Sue Miller wrote about such differences:

But that's the way it is in a family, isn't it? The stories get passed around, polished, embellished. Liddie's version or Mack's version changes as it becomes my version. And when I tell them, it's not just that the events are different but that they all mean something different too. Something I want them to mean. Or need them to. And of course, there's also the factor of time. Of how your perspective, your way of telling the story — of seeing it — changes as time passes. As you change.

Blank pages will appear now and then as an encouragement for your own notes or memories. Questions or statements follow some of the pieces as an invitation for your thoughts and reactions. For those who want to use it as such, this can be a meditation or reflection book.

You are encouraged to read and use this book as you please. It can be read from front to back. Chance selecting is also suggested. Rather than place the pieces in chronological order or in topical sections, I have chosen to place them randomly since that is how much of my writing has occurred. I didn't always write at the time something happened; at other times the heat of the moment and its effect led me to put pen to paper.

There are a few pieces written by other authors. Their or their publisher's permission has also been sought and received. They have been included to offer additional perspectives about the crossroads of life. Compare and contrast what they wrote with my accounts. I am the richer for points of view that stretch my ways of thinking and experiencing.

Thanks for your interest.

Family Pictures (1990) by Sue Miller. New York: Harper & Row, Publishers, p. 4.

Telling Secrets: A Memoir (1991) by Frederick Buechner. San Francisco: HarperCollins, p. 30.

Unexpected Writer

"*Y*ou think you are the only writer, don't you?" was the greeting from my dad that day. Said with a smile and the tone of expectancy, I curiously awaited what was to come. And out it came: a pile of yellow pages with turned-up corners, full of hand-written words, thrust in my direction by the proud writer. "Look at this," he said.

Little did I know that the written version of this man's life and legacy was now in my hands. Unbeknownst to me, my brothers, and most astoundingly, our mother, Dad had found seclusion and creativity in a writer's den he created in the storage building behind my parents' home. Steadily over a year and more, he had written his life story on these now marked and stained pages.

Even long after his death, we can take a part of him off the shelf and read.

"Would you type it for me?" he asked, inviting me to provide him with a service that would give more to the typist than either of us expected. "Yes, of course," I replied. Later, after returning home, I began to read and type this gift. Part memoir, part essay, and part sermon, the pages contained a life story of poverty, hope, the American dream, faith, and family. It was honest, poignant, and full of the man I called Dad.

I've received many things from my father over the years: ties and mugs, shirts and books, but no gift came close to matching the power of his life story. There are too many accounts of parents who keep the doors closed to shaping influences of their early years. Decisions made that changed the course of lives can be buried along with a person. In his memoir, *Growing Up*, Russell Baker described this tendency: *Children rarely want to know who their parents were before they were parents, and when age finally stirs their curiosity there is no parent left to tell them. If a parent does lift the curtain a bit, it is often only to stun the young with some exemplary tale of how much harder life was in the old days.* Fortunately, my father didn't wait until it was too late.

Dad's tale was exemplary and it did contain stories of hard living, but the intent was not to regale the reader. Even more important than the details was his action of doing the writing. Some narratives deserve more than memory. And words on paper can be read again and again. Even long after his death, we can take a part of him off the shelf and read.

What makes it all the more special was the surprise. This man was a talker, not a writer. I have very few letters or notes from him because he wrote so few. So for him to write anything, especially his memoir, took special effort and love. Some stories are hard to write because of their content. Some others are hard to write because the author has little experience putting words on paper. Somehow Dad put pencil to yellow paper, the collection of which he waved in my face that day, months after he started writing.

No, I'm not the only writer in the family. There has always been room for more. There still is. The unexpected often occurs when pen is put to paper. I can hardly wait for someone else to wave pages filled with their story, asking me to type or read.

Quote from *Growing Up* (1982) by Russell Baker. New York: Congdon & Weed, Inc., p. 6.

I did not know it at the time but my father's story was what some now call an ethical/spiritual will. Gerontologists and family educators are urging that in addition to legal and living wills, writing an ethical or spiritual will should be done. Such a will involves a looking back over one's life for lessons, insights, "ah hahs," and learnings that could be useful and valuable to peers and those who follow. An ethical/spiritual will could be done at any stage of life, but is especially important for middle-aged and older persons. (See *Ethical Wills: Putting Your Values On Paper* (2002) by Barry Baines. Cambridge: Perseus Publishing).

What are some life lessons you have learned from good or hard times? If you were to write an ethical/spiritual will or your story, what would you want to include that would reflect your values and faith?

If that seems too daunting, what is one particular lesson from your life that could be shared with others?

Torn Between Two Loves

It's not my story to tell. Still, it's too important a memory to lose, even to embellish if and when the story is told again. My son is not a writer, at least not yet. But, in a moment he became a poet, an artist, and a story-teller worthy of the ages. Twelve hundred miles away from him, but intimately linked by births, by gender, by relationship, and by joy I heard a tale of love I want to tell.

For over six hours he had been the attentive husband to his laboring wife, each contraction and release pulling them more in rhythm, closeness, and synergy. He, the dutiful and loving husband, was there to be with his bride and soon-to-be mother. The decision made to do a cesarean delivery; he stayed at his comfort station, supporting his wife in this once in a lifetime moment.

When the moment of delivery occurred, the baby girl, wiped free of protective and nurturing fluids, was offered to him. It was then the drama took for him an unexpected and poignant twist. It was the description of this moment of moments when my son became a sage to families everywhere.

The offer of his daughter was for him abrupt. Attentive to his wife for hours, she was now experiencing even more discomfort and pain as the placenta was lifted from her. Divided loyalties tugged at him as he wanted to be with his wife and also with his daughter. And that is the heart of this story. My son, more a romantic than I knew, torn between two loves, wanted desperately for his wife to share the moment he was now being offered.

I, a father and first-time grandfather, already experiencing a joy and excitement only grandparents can know, was now moved to tears as my son told me of his pulls and tugs and most of all his love for the mother of their child. That is the story to be captured. That is the story to be told.

Written at the birth of my first grandchild in 1993.

The Captain

My boss is seven-years-old. This is not a startling arrangement. Some years ago the new minister at my church was younger than I. It was then that age as an essential quality for leadership was faced and released. I had thought the older you were, the wiser. The distance from younger ministers and managers to seven-year-old bosses is not wide.

My seven-year-old grandson is the captain. I'm the first mate; he calls me Matey. He first announced this arrangement when he was four. Mine is a position of privilege because when he became the captain there were no other first mates. I remain the only one. My wife has a unique role, but she is not a first mate. She is Toots, an appreciative term for one who shows due respect to the captain and who does not interfere with the captain and his first mate.

I've had many bosses over the years, but none like the captain. He is clearer than most of my supervisors have been about plans and who is in charge. There is no boundary ambiguity; he is the captain. While we work together on some projects — abstract drawing for example — the ultimate choice of colors or theme, if there is one, is his to make. I know my place. He knows his.

While there is no pay, there are substantial benefits. My captain is a teacher. His values, preferences, and treatment of subordinates are congruent and consistent. He is more direct than most of my bosses have been. He believes that I can learn from my mistakes and successes, each of which he notes as we work together. He also affirms me with handshakes, hugs, and incredibly rich smiles or grins. Each time I work with the captain, I leave renewed and full of joy. Most important, there is a loyalty covenant between the captain and his worker that invites reciprocity.

Would-be corporate managers and aspiring organization consultants could forego MBA programs, saving time and money, by spending time with seven-year-olds. Valuable work and life lessons can be learned about balancing work and play, power, clarity of direction, of respect for those in leadership roles, and about humility. I think I'm gaining what they call life-long learning. Too bad it took a long life for this boss to arrive and offer the position.

With thanks to Liam Magistad, The Captain.

Male Tears

Tears well up from pools of pain,
Desiring to do what they are supposed to do,
Seek surface drainage.
The troubled waters exert pressure upward,
But clogged pipes,
Corroded by disuse,
Block their flow toward release.

A Man's Tears

A man's plumber resides within.
His handyman kit ready,
If and when the manhole cover is lifted
Tears well up and seek surface drainage.
Blocked by poor priming,
Inexperience,
Rocky soil,
They reluctantly return to their storage place
To await a plumber.

"Male Tears" was published in the *Journal of Pastoral Care*, Spring 1990, p. 26.

"A Man's Tears" was published in *Journal of Poetry Therapy*, 4, 2, Winter 1990, p. 130.

*T*he previous three pieces are about crossroads in my life: the birth of a grandchild, interactions with a grandchild, and two poems about my way of grieving losses.

Which of these three pieces evoked a story of yours? Write a few notes about it.

Think about a moment of birth, sickness, or death in your life and write about something you learned from those experiences.

Write about a child who has been a teacher for you, as the Captain was for me.

_____

_____

_____

_____

_____

_____

_____

_____

_____

_____

_____

_____

_____

_____

_____

_____

_____

_____

_____

_____

Words/Food For Thought: Stories

*T*he very act of storytelling, of arranging memory and invention according to the structure of the narrative, is by definition holy.

We tell stories because we love to entertain and hope to edify.

We tell stories because they fill the silence death imposes.

We tell stories because they save us.

James Carroll, author, in *Notre Dame Magazine* (Autumn 2001).

*N*ightmares awakened a young boy in the middle of the night. He cried out for his mother who quickly joined him at his bedside. He said, "I'm afraid, Mommy." She hugged him and assured him that he need not be afraid, for not only was she going to be sleeping one room away, but God was right by his side also. "Well I know God's here," insisted the boy, "but tonight I guess I just needed somebody with skin on."

From *When Faith Is Tested* (1997) by Jeffrey R. Zurheide. Minneapolis: Fortress Press, p. 5.

*I*f you look up gossip in the *Oxford English Dictionary* you find that it is derived from the words for God and sibling, and originally meant "akin to God." It was used to describe one who has contracted spiritual kinship by acting as a sponsor at baptism; one who helps "give a name to." Eric Partridge's Origins, a dictionary of etymology, tells you simply to "see God," and there you find that the word's antecedents include gospel, godspell, and "*sabha*, a village community — notoriously interrelated."

We are interrelated — whether or not we're related by blood — story is a safety valve for people who live as intimately as that; and I would argue that gossip done well can be a holy thing. It can strengthen community bonds.

From *Dakota: A Spiritual Geography* (1993) by Kathleen Norris. New York: Ticknor & Fields, p. 72.

*E*leanor and the Big Brown Buick

The other day I went to Marshall Field's department store to pick up a wedding gift. As I entered on the State Street side, I passed the first counter where they display the cosmetics and perfumes; clerks are always squirting this stuff at you. Suddenly I had a whiff of something I had not encountered for fifty years. A certain girl named Eleanor had worn that scent when we borrowed her brother's big brown Buick and went off for a hamburger near Plymouth, Ohio.

Eleanor is now somewhere in Texas, her brother is gone, I am sure the Buick is gone, and I am damned-near gone. But after fifty years, that scent took me right back to the brown Buick and Eleanor and all the rest, which was considerable.

I think everyone has had some such experience: a chance sniff, the feel of some object, a respoken word or line that one has not heard since the eighth grade. There is something in the associational, in what we call the infinite retrievability of the past. It is embedded in the senses, in the chemistry, in the cerebrum somehow; it makes computers look simple.

From *Grace Notes And Other Fragments* by Joseph Sittler. Philadelphia: Fortress Press, 1981, p. 14.

What is the place of story in your life?

The previous two pages include stories and commentary about stories. Jesus used stories/parables. Public speakers, writers, musicians, preachers, and many family members use stories. What do you think James Carroll meant when he wrote that the very act of storytelling can be holy?

_____

_____

_____

_____

_____

_____

_____

_____

_____

_____

_____

_____

_____

_____

_____

_____

_____

_____

_____

_____

What If Jesus Had a Twin?

When asked recently to officiate in the baptism of their fraternal twin children, I quickly and eagerly said yes to the parents. It was an honor to be asked to be a part of this special event by these two people I had come to admire and appreciate. It would have been an honor to be asked by anyone. The fact that they knew me, and I them, added to the esteem I felt.

Fatherly involvement would now be the norm, not a goal, don't you think?

I haven't done lots of baptisms. My special ministry does not afford as many opportunities for this and other rituals as I would like. Hence, my thoughts, as I approached this baptism, might have been those of the novice. What I was about to do was not all that common. It was to be a baptism of twin children, a boy and girl born on the same day a couple of months earlier.

I began to wonder what it would have been like if Jesus had had a twin. Had Mary and Joseph known they were facing a multiple birth, learned after some first century form of amniocentesis, would they have taken the hard, long trip to Bethlehem? Would a journey like that, even with Herod's threat, have seemed too dangerous? And even if they did go, would the inn keeper have turned them away toward the stable if he knew Mary was carrying twins? Might his heart-strings have been tugged a little more facing two births, not one?

And what of the stable and all the animals? They were used to multiple births. Most animals are born as part of litters. Maybe, the birth that night in the stable would have seemed even more ordinary to the animals if it had been twins. Some of their bellowing and crowing about interrupted sleep and intruders might have dissipated in the face of twins.

Then, what about the angels, the shepherds, and the alleged wise ones. Sometimes we think that when there is only one of something, it is more valuable. Would the shepherds have thought that way? Would they have been even more reckless about protecting their sheep and impulsively rushed off to Bethlehem to see twin children without leaving someone behind to care for the flock? Were the wise ones prepared to do Christmas shopping for two instead of one? How much myrrh and incense did they have on hand?

Fatherhood, I'm convinced, would have taken a giant leap forward had Jesus been born a twin. Joseph, the sometimes inconspicuous parent, would have had a heck of lot more parenting responsibilities with twins. Mary's arms were wide, still are according to some. We have known that for centuries. But, Joseph would have had to carry, change, and cuddle one of the two a lot more than with only one. Fatherly involvement would now be the norm, not a goal, don't you think?

And what about fraternal twins, male and female? Boy, that would have, oops I should add, girl, that would have changed things! I'm guessing we wouldn't be debating inclusive language the way we do if Jesus had had a sister. Gender relations would be significantly altered. Wow! Even a lot of the carols we now sing would have to be re-written. King of kings and all those lines would have to be dropped or just be one of the verses. It would have been back to the drawing board for poor Handel, two Messiahs, not one. Try a double "Glory in the highest," George.

What a difference two, not one, would have made! The thought of it sure got me going. But, even two might be too few for God. My faith tells me that each of us is made in the image of God, that just as Jesus did, we are to embody God's love and make it known throughout the world. We are to mirror the love of God, like looking at a twin or having someone know your thoughts almost as quick as you do. In that sense, Jesus has a lot of brothers and sisters already. The thought that the two I was to baptize were fraternal twins made that easier to believe. I'm not sure I'm up to being an identical twin with Jesus. Fraternal would be hard enough! But, I'm willing to give it a try. I hope the two baptized will be willing also.

Fatherhood

Is it something one assumes,
        becomes,
        or earns?

Does it happen at conception,
        birth,
        acknowledgment,
        or at the moment of choice?

Who confers it,
        the child,
        society,
        the other parent,
        oneself?

Once begun,
Does it continue?
Is it temporary?
Does it come and go?
Can one be more of,
Yes, even less of a father?
How will I know when I become one?
Tell me how it feels.
How does one prepare?

Questions,
Gushing from deep inside
As boys becoming men becoming boys
Add to their collection
A role so awesome
The strongest can cringe in fright
For which the weakest muster and
Discover courage never felt before.

Fatherhood:
Whether birth, step, gay, adoptive, grand or foster
Can
When assumed
     chosen
     or acknowledged,
Not to mention
If earned or conferred,
Become
     the most humbling,
        curious,
        unpredictable,
        exciting,
        demanding,
        giving,
        liberating
Experience
Known to man. (*begun in 1984*)

*Y*ears ago, humorist Erma Bombeck wrote a column about the "real parent." Such a parent, according to Bombeck, was the one who was there for children no matter their biological or official relationship. Reflect on your thoughts about what it takes to be a "real parent."

_____

_____

_____

_____

_____

_____

_____

_____

_____

_____

_____

_____

_____

_____

_____

_____

_____

_____

_____

_____

_____

_____

_____

_____

Memory Lapses and Dignity: Handle With Care

Grocery stores thrive on memory lapses. You walk through an aisle, see something familiar and appealing, perhaps even essential, and then you try to remember if there is one of those at home. Acting on the "better safe than sorry" principle, you elect to allow the syrup, lettuce, crackers, or olive oil accompany you home. The odds are high that once there you will discover duplicates of many of your choices.

Replay this scenario, but add some degree of memory loss as a result of dementia, a stroke, or brain injury. Mix with one of those a lifetime pattern of family responsibility and an always be prepared attitude. The result can be what in most households would be called stockpiling or preparing for a rainy day — but in a household containing a matriarch with dementia, would be called a problem.

Add to this picture a room, at least a nook or cranny, one of those multi-purpose areas that, no matter the size of the house or apartment, seem to be set aside for storage; the place for those items that just don't quite fit somewhere else. Locate this area near the kitchen. Fill any and all available spaces with boxes, cans, and bottles and you can begin to picture the cache of food my mother, whose memory is failing her, has brought home out of love and dedication for her family — only after standing in a grocery store aisle wondering if one of these is at home.

Now, what started out as a memory lapse and a better safe than sorry attitude, are over the edge of acceptability, even health — many items are past-dated — and a source of embarrassment. It is not two bags of flour; it is six, not a few rolls of paper towels but what appears to be a virtual caseload.

Understandable behavior, yes, but, any act of clean-up can and will involve the intersection of the public and private sphere of a parent's life. Each of us has our own idiosyncratic stashes. For some it is chocolate, others old phonograph records, past newspapers, or one's version of the *National Geographic*. For many people living with dementia, their items are as necessary or desirable as yours or mine. It's the volume that is out of control. The result is that what was personal and somewhat private becomes public when family or others intervene. Who wants someone cleaning up their private messes?

Clean-up will also heighten the tension between independence and loss of power. Loss of memory is often only the latest of losses. Further, loss overload is the elder person's plight in too many cases. Grief can become chronic and depression an every day occurrence if not careful. My mom said to me that it was wonderful to live as long as she has, outliving her mother's and grandmother's ages already. And it had been, she added, a full and rich life, but the recent losses were the hardest.

The result is that what was personal and somewhat private becomes public when family or others intervene. Who wants someone cleaning up their private messes?

For this son and others like me, the desire to be helpful, even to take away "dangerous" items in the stash, must be balanced with appreciation for pride and self-respect: a not so easy balance. There are those who will advise that you must do what you have got to do. There are others who are more laid-back, evaluating what, if any, harm is being done. The tension grows when there is not another in the household to monitor the safety factor, especially in food preparation.

It's ironic that our family was a grocery store family, moving from a Ma and Pa operation to being part of a small but successful chain of independent stores. The grocery store dominated my early years, all the way to college and beyond. Now, almost thirty years after Dad and Mom retired from that important work, groceries again loom largely in my interactions with them. When I was younger, we brought home the stories, troubles, and joys of each day at the store, leaving the groceries back at the store. Now, there is a room at home that is a small grocery store.

*T*his is the first of several pieces about my mother and about Alzheimer's Disease. What were your reactions to this story?

Do you know someone who has lost abilities because of injury, illness, or accident? What is your story?

Add your opinion about the balance of dignity and respect with safety for those with limitations.

_____

_____

_____

_____

_____

_____

_____

_____

_____

_____

_____

_____

_____

_____

_____

_____

_____

_____

_____

_____

_____

_____

_____

Care with Words

The reason I speak to them in parables is that "seeing they do not perceive, and hearing they do not listen, nor do they understand." (Matthew 13: 13)

Words and eggs must be handled with care.
Once broken they are impossible
things to repair. (Sexton)

The same word can be humble at one moment and arrogant the next. And a humble word can be transformed easily and imperceptibly into an arrogant one, whereas it is a difficult and protracted process to transform an arrogant word into one that is humble. (Havel)

This is a book of words! As a lover of words — whether in essay, poems, letters, or fiction — I stand in awe of words. I have heard it said about one writer that he only spoke in a whisper because of his keen sense of the power words have. He thought it wise to avoid being too bold with his choice and use of words. I have often wanted to join with him. Perhaps, that is one of the reasons that much of my writing has been brief and many pieces have been written in a parable or story form. Short pieces invite more attention to the words used. Further, they encourage one not to say or write everything that could be said or written.

Wendell Berry, in his poem "Words" (the full poem follows), also seemed to question his use of words. The poem begins:

What is one to make of a life given
to putting things into words,
saying them, writing them down?

Perhaps, he then mused, it would be wiser to stop, be quiet, take note, and experience rather than rush to put words to the world around us. As I read this, two of the loves of my life appeared to be in conflict, a dichotomy of opposing peak parts of my life. I love words and I also love solitude in natural settings. I wondered where Berry's poem was going. Then, Berry returned, in his provocative and enchanting poem, to suggest that a human tendency, perhaps even responsibility, is to name and tell the story.

What do you think? What is your opinion about words and their uses and misuses? And in moments of awareness of your surrounding world, when is it better to be quiet and when is it better to put your experience into words... whether said or written? Here is the Berry poem, a possible resource for your thoughts.

"A Word About Words," from *Open letters: Selected Writings 1965-1990* by Vaclav Havel (1992). New York: Vintage Books, p. 388.

The Awful Rowing Toward God by Anne Sexton (1975). Boston: Houghton Mifflin Company, p. 71

Words

1.

What is one to make of a life given

to putting things into words,

saying them, writing them down?

Is there a world beyond words?

There is. But don't start, don't

go on about the trees unqualified,

standing in light that shines

to time's end beyond its summoning

name. Don't praise the speechless

starlight, the unspeakable dawn.

Just stop.

2.

Well, we can stop

for a while, if we try hard enough,

if we are lucky, let the phoebe, the sycamore,

the river, the stone call themselves

by whatever they call themselves, their own

sounds, their own silence, and thus

may know for a moment the nearness

of the world, its vastness,

its vast variousness, far and near,

which only silence knows. And then

we must call all things by name

out of the silence again to be with us,

or die of namelessness.

What One Seems

I   *Sometime since then and there*
               The dreams,
               Planted as perennials,
               Turned out to be annuals instead.

II   *Sometime between there and then and here and now*
               The rules changed
               While play continued.
               The man I am
               Chose not to be the man I had envisioned.
               The game goes on.

III   *Sometimes in the midst of here and now*
               My there and then shows up.
               Generations appear in one body.
               I listen attentively,
               Wondering which will speak first.

IV   *The man I am*
               Can, from this distance, see
               Ways the boy I was got here.
               The boy, looking ahead,
               Would have thought this man strange.

After reading my poem, "What One Seems," read the prayer below by Thomas Merton. Then, write some of your thoughts and reactions to either or both.

My Lord God, I have no idea where I am going. I do not see the road ahead of me. I cannot know for certain where it will end. Nor do I really know myself, and the fact that I think that I am following your will does not mean that I am actually doing so. But I believe that the desire to please you does in fact please you.

_____

_____

_____

_____

_____

_____

_____

_____

_____

_____

_____

_____

_____

_____

_____

_____

_____

_____

_____

_____

_____

_____

Birthmates

*C*all it coincidence, fate, serendipity, or the hand of God. Who knows? Strange, nevertheless, that while I was being born in a North Carolina house where an airport is now, another person was beginning her life 1200 miles away in Minnesota. Neither of us nor our families were aware that over 35 years later we would meet, become friends individually and with our partners, share birthdays, weddings, children, holidays, walks in the woods, faith, books, food, and her cancer. There is nothing unique about meeting people from next door or across the world and finding much in common. There is something, however, very special about a birth mate with whom you share so much. I have only one birth mate that I know. Out of the thousands of people in the world who started life on March 18, 1943, it was hers and mine whose life paths crossed. Now she has cancer.

I don't experience her cancer as would her twin, if she had one, as do her siblings, son, or her dear husband, even other friends. My experience is mine alone, at times too alone, but never as solitary as her present journey. As the old spiritual says, she must walk it by herself, as must I, knowing, as we both do, that we are or can be surrounded by others, including each other, any time we desire it.

I hope she knows that my birthday became even more special when I had someone with whom to share it. I hope she knows that Methodists and Moravians have had a special connection for a long time, beginning with Wesley and that famous ship ride to America. We are among the keepers of that legacy. I hope she knows that she has become a part of me, that she has influenced me in her care for the natural world, her mid-life plunge into icons, her love of tradition, her desire for right words for the right time for the gathered people, and her quiet strength. I hope she knows that those learnings and more will not die but will live on in me and countless others. And I hope she knows that she is teaching me about living and dying so that I can do both with the degree of the courage, dignity, and serenity that she demonstrates day after day.

I wish the cancer was dying, not her. I wish birthmates could give bone marrow because everyone born on March 18, 1943 had something in their blood and bones nobody else had which would stop her cancer. We probably do have something special inside, at least she and I. We just don't know how to recognize or use it, except, in the passing of the peace, the peace that passes all understanding, even cancer, even dying too soon, for now and evermore.

The cancer is now dead. She is not. Yes, someone will say, and it will be accurate, that she died sometime between six and six-thirty, July 22, 1993, but, she still lives. Resurrection can take many forms, one of which occurs when someone leaves indelible marks inside you that live on in spite of their death. She did.

It's more than my reluctance to think that she's dead. I, like many, expect to hear her voice, to have her join our conversation, or to offer a cookie anytime now. But, those are more than transition fantasies. This belief is more than a nostalgic addition to my array of heroes and heroines. Living and dying will never be the same again because of her. Nor will they be separated as far from each other as I used to want them to be. Mortality, she reminded me, brings with it special responsibilities for service, joy, and keen appreciation for each moment. The rest of my days will be enriched because of the seasoning she added to my life. Resurrection is not something to be taken lightly.

Resurrection can take many forms, one of which occurs when someone leaves indelible marks inside you that live on in spite of their death.

Going Public

If courage is a manly virtue, one that men supposedly possess through masculine transmission from one generation to another, there was a break in my synapses last night. I was scared; excited too. I knew it would be a night to remember. Last night my son and I taught together for the first time. That in itself would be special. The night was all the more memorable and emotional because we approached our material through personal stories and discussion of related issues. We were invited to lead a family sociology course at my son's university in a discussion of separation, divorce, and remarriage. My son is currently an undergraduate. It was a topic we both knew intimately from direct experience. There was no rehearsal. I didn't know in advance what my son would say, nor did he have a preview of my personal stories. He did know some of the material I would introduce in the issue portion of the class. We had only agreed on our general outline and an order of presentations.

I was proud for the moment, thrilled at the idea, excited about the possibility, and scared to death.

The idea for leading the session had sounded intriguing, fun, and a rare opportunity when we discussed doing it a year or so earlier. My son was taking the course at that time. We discussed his texts, the subjects covered, some of the issues being addressed, in the midst of which, one of us had the wild idea that we could teach the session, divorce and remarriage. He would take the child's perspective, I the father's.

Maybe we said it because the conversation about the family course had provoked discussion once again of our own memories of my marital separation sixteen years earlier and its effects on my son, his brother, me, and all the others involved. It was a continuing topic; this was just the latest episode. Wounds created by marital chasms take long to close and heal. Indeed, it is never done. Reminders arrive periodically, often unanticipated and unannounced, and won't leave until more grieving occurs. Divorce, I have come to believe, results in chronic grief, especially for children. In any case, an idea tossed onto the table was quickly transformed into an invitation by my son's teacher and a date was logged into our calendars.

As last night approached, I became simultaneously apprehensive and exhilarated. I knew I would be experiencing something too few parents ever do, something few even desire. I knew also that my son does not mince his words. While I frequently have wished that he would share more words through letters and phone calls to me, I knew that he had come to place a value on honest words that would not be compromised, even in this public forum. I was scared. Simultaneously, I took it as a great compliment that my son was willing to do this with me. Going public about your memories and experience of your parents' separation and divorce and doing it with your old man present, co-leading the class with you, is not high, I would guess, on the desired activity list of most college seniors. I was proud for the moment, thrilled at the idea, excited about the possibility, and scared to death.

When it was over, some friends and family members asked me how it had gone. "Did you enjoy it?" someone asked. Enjoy? No. Am I glad it happened, that we did it? You bet! It was an event to treasure. Was it hard to do? Yes. My son, as I had expected, did talk about some of the more difficult and painful experiences for him following the marital separation and subsequent divorce. While he did not say anything I had not heard in earlier versions, it was still difficult to hear them said publicly. He did not attack me or put me down. He simply said it like it was for him. That, his classmates needed to hear. That was our reason for being there, to share our particular window on divorce in the hope that our story might aid them in understanding and addressing some of the issues for families going through divorce, including their own.

The issues were personal, specific, and universal. My son talked about his sense of betrayal that his idealized family would suddenly end when his parents separated. He talked about his anger at our failure to include him and his older brother in the loop earlier than we did. He talked about the difficulty of adjusting to two homes, one 1200 miles away from the other, and also 1200 miles away from his friends, toys, and bicycle. I tried to listen — and I did — as his father and the co-leader of the class. Even though we were covering familiar ground, my son was once again reminding me, and those willing to hear, about the emotional costs to children of parental divorce. Even when the decision to divorce continues to seem right, even if the child believes it to be a wise choice, the pain can still remain. An adult decision left its mark on my son. The healing continues.

I, too, shared my story. We invited questions and got many. I provided some perspective from the literature on divorce with the class. The students and the teacher thanked us. The session came to an end.

As we left, I hugged my son in appreciation and relief. I had received a gift from him. I wanted him to know I had gotten it. I thanked him also for his courage. It had helped me face my fear. We had adapted several male rules and traditions by speaking openly about our feelings and experiences. We had drawn on courage to talk openly about personal matters. We spoke to each other even as we spoke to the class. Yes, the divorce has left its marks. We were also making other marks; ones that will linger for a long, long time.

𝒲rite your reactions to this story. Is there a particular section or line that grabbed your attention? If so, what occurred to you?

There is a long history of stories about wounded healers. People who have experienced wounds can either stay angry the rest of their lives or they can transform their wounds by finding in their experiences insights for continued living. Such acts are not avoidance or denial of the wound and its causes. Rather, wounded healers are those who seek to find meaning from painful life events.

I believe that my son and I were trying to become wounded healers that night at his university class. Reflect on your experiences as a wounded healer.

_____

_____

_____

_____

_____

_____

_____

_____

_____

_____

_____

_____

_____

_____

_____

_____

_____

_____

AN INTRODUCTION TO THIS POEM

If I was forced to choose only one poem for sharing with others at this time (2006), I would choose the following one. When I first read it, I knew immediately that it was special! Few poems have evoked the strong personal reaction it did and still does each time I read it privately or in public.

It is a poem by the South African poet, Ingrid de Kok. She wrote it, capturing her experience of the opening of the Truth and Reconciliation Commission in that country in 1996.

Read it. Read it aloud; poems are often best read out loud. Note your reactions and responses in thought or by writing in the margins or on this page.

Leave a bit of time and then read some additional information and commentary provided following the poem.

The Archbishop Chairs the First Session

The Truth and Reconciliation Commission,
April 1996, East London, South Africa

On the first day
after a few hours of testimony
the Archbishop wept.
He put his grey head
on the long table
of paper and protocols
and he wept.

The national
and international cameramen
filmed his weeping,
his misted glasses,
his sobbing shoulders,
the call for a recess.

It doesn't matter what you thought
of the Archbishop before or after,
of the settlement, the commission,
or what the anthropologists flying in
from less studied crimes and sorrows
said about his discourse,
or how many doctorates,
books and installations followed,
or even if you think this poem
simplifies, lionizes,
romanticizes, mystifies.

There was a long table, starched purple vestment
and after a few hours of testimony,
the Archbishop, chair of the commission,
laid down his head, and wept.

That's how it began.

From *Terrestrial Things: Poems* (2002) by Ingrid de Kok. Capetown, South Africa: Kwela/Snailpress, p. 22. Reprinted with permission of the author.

I have heard it told that Bishop Tutu, immediately after putting his head down and crying, regretted doing so. He feared that because of his position his actions would detract from the testimony of the citizens of South Africa who had told or would be telling their stories to the commission. To the contrary he was told. Many of those there to tell of horrible violence to one or more of their family members said to him that they had been hoping and waiting for years for someone in authority to show such compassion and understanding of their losses.

I have thought that this poem is like a parable. It is more than the description of one man and a very public act of sympathy and grief. It is a parable about the yearning for caring responses to private and public tragedies. It is also a parable about leadership in the face of horrible accounts of real experiences. I yearn for such leaders given so much violence throughout the world. I pray for such courage when someone tells me of their pain.

To My Children, I Pledge...

(This was first written in 1992 and published by the St. Paul Pioneer Press, *that Father's Day weekend. While a bit of it is dated — the men's movement was at its height — the core content has stood the test of time).*

A few weeks ago, some colleagues and I led a three-generational men's retreat. Toward the end, the sons were separated from their fathers and grandfathers. The task of the fathers and grandfathers was to decide on messages they wanted to give to their sons. They were asked: If something should happen to you on the way home, what would you want your sons to have heard from you? What are the most important things you can say to your sons? What do you want your sons to remember as your legacy to them?

The sons, for their part, got the rare opportunity to prepare advice for fathers. What did they, boys and young men ages 12 to 20, want to say to fathers and grandfathers, more importantly, to *their* fathers and grandfathers about fatherhood?

The separate groups, after working on the tasks, reunited to share their results. Passions were high, as both had taken their assignments seriously and both had agreed on one or two primary messages. Each was prepared without any awareness of what the other group might say.

This is what the sons told the fathers: Tell us what you believe and stand for. Tell us your guiding principles. Let us grow, and while doing so, give us some slack. Let us make our choices — guided, yes, by your input and your values — but regardless of what choices we make, don't ever abandon us. Hang in there with us — no matter what.

The fathers' and grandfathers' two messages to their sons: We love you, sons, and we are proud of you.

Thinking back over that retreat, and about the growing discussions of fatherhood and families, and about the messages I got from my dad and grandfather, and especially about what I want to say to my sons and daughter, I have composed the following pledges. They are personal, but I wrote them with all fathers in mind — because whatever I choose to say to my children can be reinforced and enriched if the friends of my children hear similar things from their fathers.

Look over my list, and see what you think. Which pledges would you add to my list? What steps do you need to take to improve or restore your relationships with your children? Children tell me what they want more than anything else this Father's Day is to know that their dads really care about them. I plan to make sure mine hear that from me.

1. I pledge that I will never, ever abandon you! Regardless of any differences you and I may have, and regardless of any differences your mother and I have, I will never, ever abandon you! You can count on my support.

2. I pledge that I will tell you about your history. I will teach you our family heritage, stories, rituals, and traditions. I want you to be proud of yourself and your peoples. Even though our family's history includes some painful episodes, I want you to know you are special.

3. I pledge to teach you about strength by being honest and respectful of you and your friends and by expecting you to do the same for me and them. Strength of character is a lot more important than brute force, thick skin, or tough talk.

4. I pledge to you that I will keep no friends with whom you should feel unsafe. He or she is no friend of mine who would do you harm.

5. I pledge to honor you and your body by showing respect for yours, and anyone else's in our home. Sexuality is more than body parts or genital contact. Sexuality has to do with how you carry yourself around both sexes. Sexuality has to do with relationships.

6. I pledge to show you the value of work by working on my marriage, by working for causes, by working on my relationship with you, by working for a living as long as I am able, and by continual efforts to live my faith, which is the hardest work of all.

7. I pledge to you that my discipline will never be violent or abusive.

8. I pledge you my love and my pride. Just as I always want you to know that I am proud to be your father, I want you also to be proud of me — and, most important, I want you to be proud of yourself.

Write some words or lines of pledges you might make to someone dear to you.

_____

_____

_____

_____

_____

_____

_____

_____

_____

_____

_____

_____

_____

_____

_____

_____

_____

_____

Spirit of God

Spirit of God, this is my wailing song
Hear all my cries, sadness fills my voice
Teach me to listen, help me live with loss
Sorrow follows everywhere I go

Spirit of God, they say you know my grief
So then, come close, enfold me with your care
My heart is heavy, yearning for relief
Carry my burden, it's more than I can bear

Spirit of God, I've heard your people's tales
Abraham, Martha, yes, and Peter too
They, too, were tested, hopes and dreams assailed
You did not leave them, You made life anew

Spirit of God, descend upon my heart
Help me find peace in ways new and tried
When sorrows linger, creative let me be
Open my eyes to find You at my side

Lyrics of grief written to the familiar tune — *Morecambe*

The Applause Mine

Portions of a Letter From Father to Son

Eighteen, almost nineteen years after your birth, I face the prospect of my first born graduating from high school. Such an event gives this father pause... a time to reflect on wishes of days past, on the man you've become, and the parent I've been.

I know one thing for sure. I am proud of the boy/man you have become, but not pride in the sense of taking credit. No, I'm proud of who you are, for what you believe, how you behave, and what you value. Given the hurdles of parental divorce, parents separated by 1200 miles, moves from city to city, your own continuing difficulties to overcome learning challenges while not being labeled by school or peers, as well as all the regular stuff kids face as they grow and change, I am all the more impressed by your accomplishments. In spite of the stresses, you have been friendly and accessible to adults and peers alike. You have balanced jobs and school, friends and family. You have been a trustworthy and hard-working employee in several jobs. You have developed and kept friendships, a not-so-easy accomplishment these days. You have reached for excellence, best exemplified by reaching the state tournament in wrestling. And you have identified and held values that show respect for others, for your own body, and for yourself. For all that and more, I am proud and happy and filled with awe and love.

There is a tendency for parents to take the credit if a child does well or blame the child if otherwise. I would like to think I have been an influence on you. However, you have for many years made many of the important decisions affecting you and will continue to do so. The credit is therefore yours; the joy and applause mine.

From *The Northfield Magazine*, vol.4, no. 1, 1990

Father's Day

I have no Father's Day Card to send this year!

Even though I stood and read the many choices

At many racks, in many stores, many times

I have not signed my name or written a message

This year.

My father died 36 days ago!

What does one do when habits and traditions

Lose their reason?

Does one send a card to all the fathers he sees,

To the sons who have become fathers,

To the surrogates that have been father-like,

To the dead father who might still be listening,

To the muse that links fathers to sons to fathers and their sons,

Or to the mom that shared life with the man for 68 years?

Does anyone have an answer or response?

One of my condolence cards called me an orphan

An odd label for one as old as me.

Others wrote of my longevity genes

A dad of 93 is not yet common

Whatever I am, I am lonely

I miss him and the ritual of cards

I don't like standing in stores unsure of the etiquette.

One day a year or so from now

I won't be stopping at the card rack

At this time of year.

Until then, the card rack is grief permitted

But without social supports

Without manly choices

Except to purchase or walk away.

I, a man, a son, a father

Lingered

Pondering a ritual and habit now ending

With no champagne or graveyard nearby.

I, like years past, looked for a card for my dad!

Written in 2005, following my father's death.

After my father died, I was reminded of a ritual he and I shared for over 60 years, the ritual of Father's Day cards. Writing about my grief and the ritual reaffirmed for me the importance of many routine but significant gestures and practices. Write a bit about an important ritual for you, one still being practiced or one you miss sharing with someone now gone from your life.

In a poem, "The Gathering," Wendell Berry wrote about the intergenerational connections between parents and children. He, as I have done in the two previous poems, focused on the ties between fathers and sons. Each of my pieces attempts to give tribute to what I have gained from my father and one of my sons. What are some things you have gained from those close to you?

See *The Country of Marriage* (1975) by Wendell Berry. New York: Harcourt Brace Joanovich, Publishers, p. 32, for "The Gathering."

Pilgrimage Home

I called my mom this evening

Nothing new, this Sunday ritual

Long ago, calls became our weekend routine

Like before, we exchanged greetings,

News, love, and what we were doing

Then, her consistent exclamation

"This call made my day"

Sadness followed

Not because our call was brief

Nor due to the distance between us

No, my mom won't remember this call

Usually this does not distress me

For years now, we have shared her Alzheimer's

Tonight, however, I wanted her to remember Iona

Iona, place of memory, island of history

Land of deep roots

I wanted Mom to know I was here

For centuries, pilgrims have come and gone

From this hard and lovely place

Her pilgrimage is almost over

She has come to the edge of being gone

Still her delight when I told her Sunday

Will be similar to the joy

When I tell her on Wednesday where I am

Sometimes pilgrims need neither a history

Nor a destination

Sometimes moments of delight suffice

I came to Iona to learn something

I did,

Now, I remember,

Call home

That's where all pilgrimages begin

A slightly different version of this poem appeared in *Fire and Bread* (2007) edited by Ruth Burgess. Glasgow: Wild Goose Publications, p. 244.

Begun at Iona Abbey, September 2005. Iona is an island off the west coast of Scotland.

Gift Leaves Reflection of a Valued Friend

We connected first as men interested in men's issues, fatherhood, childcare, and writing. Soon after we discovered our mutual love of cooking and eating good food, travel, music, small parties, sparkling conversations, and San Francisco. Our connection quickly found common ground around professionalism, high standards, and integrity.

We discovered differences also. He was opinionated, often to the point of verging on tactlessness. I was the conflict manager, trying to smooth over differences. He thrived on control and direction, thereby maintaining the high standards he believed in; I reached for the same goal through discussion, teaming, and moderating. He desired transparency; I was more tolerant of ambiguity. He was gay; I heterosexual. He was not overtly religious, though strangely spiritual; I was the theologically trained family professional and clergyman still active in my denomination.

The differences spiced our friendship. I'm the richer for the challenges of finding a soul mate so different than I.

He was one of the first to affirm my writing, to encourage it, to expect me to put pen to paper. He heard my voice and served as an amplifier through his journal so that others could hear. He gave meaning to the word "nurturing," using it as part of the title for a men's journal before nurturing men was popular or faddish. I shared with him some of his joy and pain of being a pioneer. My writing took off because of his confidence in me for what I could say.

Three years ago, he told me about the HIV virus. Last year he was diagnosed with AIDS. That took a lot of the joy out of the ride.

Three weeks after I wrote those words, my friend died. His ride ended. Even so, our friendship goes on. Friends don't vanish when they are not there, especially those of the soul mate variety. People who become influential linger with us in ways we hardly fathom. Frederick Buechner wrote once that, "Memory is more than a looking back at a time that is no longer; it is a looking out into another kind of time altogether where everything that ever was continues not just to be, but to grow and change with the life that is in it still. The people we loved. The people who loved us. The people who, for good or ill, taught us things."

Before he died, my friend asked me if I would like anything of his. I most wanted his life, but he and I both knew that would be taken from us soon. So, our goodbyes included talk of stuff, stuff of his I might like.

Another friend of mine has a name for those kinds of things. He calls them "worthies," to connote the power of legacy, of memory or example they become. I knew what worthies were. I had some. A few years ago my father gave me a pocket watch that has been held by six generations of Bowman men. Each time I touch it, even see it, I think of the men of my life and what I have been given and what I have taken from them. Buechner is right, memory is more than a looking back.

There is beauty in the world that is accessible to me because he showed me how to see.

So, I looked around my friend's house, knowing more powerfully with each step that, yes, I did want something. Today, almost a year past his death, I have in front of me a glass paperweight. In it are colors and shapes that serve instantly to remind me of my friend. There is beauty in the world that is accessible to me because he showed me how to see. His eyes may now be closed; mine have been opened.

I want somehow to open other eyes, eyes now closed to seeing homosexuals as whole human beings, as neighbors deserving of every right and privilege of any citizen. I get frustrated and angry when I read and hear statements against gays and lesbians, disguised or overt, because such statements remind me of what my friend and so many others have had to put up with. The paperweight reminds me of his oppression as well as our friendship. I dream that others would have such a friend as I did. I dream that those who are quick to attack gays would, before speaking, think whether they would say or do the same thing were their child, brother, or best friend gay. Prejudice is easy until you know someone who is what you are prejudiced against.

So, I take pen to paper as my friend encouraged, as he would want me to do. And I keep writing. I want to be worthy of the friendship his paperweight represents. Joyously, I take friends, like him, along with me.

The Buechner quote is from *The Sacred Journey* (1982) New York: Harper & Row, Publishers.

This is a slightly adapted version of a guest column that appeared in the *Star Tribune* March 15, 1993.

*T*hink of someone in your life who is different in some significant way from you. How do you celebrate your differences? How do you transcend the differences and find common ground?

Biblical stories in the older and newer testaments often include people who are different in some way from their society, yet whom God or Jesus included or embraced. What do such stories mean to you?

_____

_____

_____

_____

_____

_____

_____

_____

_____

_____

_____

_____

_____

_____

The following poem was first published in 1991. Fourteen years later,
I added two verses to the poem in response to a call for poets and
writers to address themes of home and homelessness for an exhibition
in Minneapolis and Saint Paul, Minnesota. My revised poem was
selected for inclusion. The initial stanza is here, followed on the next
pages by the newer additions. You are invited on the writing page that
follows to write a bit about there and then and here and now.

Safe Places

As children
Our games included safe places:
Bases where we were safe and free;
Lines that the monster intruder could not cross;
Areas off limits, out of the games;
Parents around whose legs we wrapped ourselves yelling,
"You can't get me, I'm safe here!"

Now older
I'm still looking for safe places.
But, the fears inside
Seem to know the safe places I seek.
They wait there patiently for my arrival,
Courage and faith, my only legs left to stand on.

From the Fall 1991 issue of *Voices: The Art And Science Of Psychotherapy*

Imagined Places

(stanza two)

As children
Our games included imagined places
Where, for as long as the game lasted,
We were smart, strong, and in charge.
In those brief moments
Possibilities overcame barriers;
The world was ours.

Now older
I still play the same game
Hoping that before my time expires
I can be smarter, stronger, and in charge
Just long enough for
Imagination to open its doors
Inviting me through.

Home Places

(stanza three)

As children
We played house.
Sometimes I was the father,
Sometimes a child,
Sometimes a teacher or cop.
House was wherever we were playing.
We didn't play home; we played house,

Now older
I know that home is more than place.
Still... place,
A loving place,
Place that you can count on
Makes home easier.
I hope my children will play house
In their homes.

Can be found in *Home Sweet Home Again: An Exhibition of Art and Poetry* (2005),
Published by *Family Housing Fund,* Minneapolis, pp. 10-11.

Royalty

The man sitting alone in the restaurant
Had he asked for service for one
Attention to be paid only him

And, if so, had the wait staff cleared the restaurant
Quickly disbursing confused diners
Giving him the privacy he desired

Or had he come in at the wrong hour
One of those in-between-sittings times

Or did the locals know something about this place
The stranger could not know until after eating

Whatever the reason
He sat like a king receiving the services
A man of his status deserved

Some years earlier, after a glorious concert in Amsterdam,
My wife and I stopped at a restaurant
Only to see the staff closing down for the evening
As we turned to leave, the owner escorted us back inside
The staff returned to their appointed stations
As we two received their elegant and unhurried care
The only customers to be seen

Everyone should be a king or queen at least for one meal
Everyone should sit tall like the solitary man
Like the couple enthralled earlier with music
Filled in due course with hospitality flavored food
Flushed with wonderful embarrassment
Everyone deserves their moment of royalty

Solitary Man,
I hereby pronounce you are King for a Day!

Begun in St. Louis while passing a large restaurant.

Subdued Hooting

My son called the other day and said he had finally found a job. I screamed inside with relief and exhilaration while exclaiming to him my joy at this welcome and yearned-for-news. Four months since graduation from a university; four months from the promise I and the American people had made to him that, if he worked hard and got a college degree, doors would open; four months from joy at getting a bachelor's degree followed by frustrating weekly reminders that the degree meant little toward finding a job, a real job, I could hardly contain myself at the announcement a job was his!!! I have faced and still face the fear that one day I could be without employment, without a secure job. It is a scare that still rattles my male sense of security and self-esteem. I had not, however, counted as one of my parental roles and responsibilities the sleepless nights and preoccupation when one of your progeny searches for and does not find a job. It has been as or more painful than watching my wee ones fall off a bike repeatedly while trying to learn to balance a moving vehicle that seemed out of your control.

My son had a job! I wanted to scream with thanksgiving to the gods of business, security, and parenting.

Then, he told me the job was with Hooters — a restaurant chain with a reputation for as much or more attention to women's breasts than their chicken wings, and, in some settings, for harassment of female employees.

We talked about Hooters, about exploitation of women, about their written policies, about his relief at finding a job, one with management training built-in, about freedom of wait-staff and customers in choosing jobs and places to eat, about symbols, and about his mounting bills.

I wanted to scream again... a different scream. Joy, I cried, should not have to have a mixer of conscience and morality... not now, not me, not my son. But, it did. It always does.

It was and is my son's decision. Even so, I shared with him my happiness and my concern. I was troubled that I felt compelled to talk as I did. I wanted desperately to pop the champagne of celebration with no hesitation, no trepidation. I wanted for him and for me a moment without scrutiny, of unadulterated joy. It was not to be. Too many fathers have failed to talk with their sons about female exploitation.

I had not, however, counted as one of my parental roles and responsibilities the sleepless nights and preoccupation when one of your progeny searches for and does not find a job.

Twelve hundred miles apart is too far for such conversations. I yearned to give him a hug, to talk with him in person. I know him to be honest and forthright, even to his own detriment at times. I paused and thought of the other businesses in which he might have found employment, "respectable" places like banks and insurance companies, which sometimes cover up their values, or disguise their earnings at our expense. Least offensive, should not, I thought, be the primary lens of scrutiny when looking for jobs.

Parents, or more accurately this parent, can easily hope for purity, more purity, than I found. This episode shattered whatever was left of my parental innocence, shattered it like all the earlier times, before I was ready. My son probably has lost some innocence also. Yet, I want to hold onto it for him. I want him to move from college to the work world open and unencumbered by scandal or lack of congruence. I would like more ease in the transition. No doubt, he is probably more ready for the "real world" than I was at his age or am for him now. It is I who probably needs the hug more than he. He could probably give a hoot about my musings. This is my hard lesson for the week. I think I will pray and hope for strength. Parenting adult children is not easy.

*T*his reflection addresses, among other themes, the tension that occurs when value differences are present in relationships. It is not always easy to share such differences while maintaining the connections. I described one incident in my life with one of my sons. Is there a moment in your life that also deserves discerning thought? What is it?

_____

_____

_____

_____

_____

_____

_____

_____

_____

_____

_____

_____

_____

_____

_____

_____

_____

_____

_____

_____

_____

_____

_____

_____

_____

Glee to Start the Day

*T*he glee of a ninety-one-year-old man who, five days late, has just had a bowel movement, is unmatchable, its only comparison, the toddler who has achieved similar success. Toothless, rubbing the sleep out of his eyes, but with a gleam on his face, my dad slowly moved around the corner of the kitchen and announced his overnight success. His grin and delight filled the kitchen and caressed this son who had worried most of the night how the next day would begin. Dad announced with gusto that he had almost awoken Mom and me at 3:00 a.m. with the news of his release. And then, showing the depth of meaning this event had for this aging man, he reported that he had reached into the toilet just to touch what he had waited so long to see. He firmly hugged me, his smile wrapped around my body, and proclaimed that I could fix whatever I wanted for the family breakfast. He would not be in charge; I was the chief cook, for at least one day. And off he went to dress for his best day in a long time.

And I'm confident that had I chosen that day to talk with my father about my almost sixty year old body, he would have listened without embarrassment or distress.

Caregiving children need such moments to remind them that basic bodily functions frequently dominate the daily lives for many elders. We, who often know so little of marathon constipation, still have most of our own teeth, can rise out of chairs with relative ease, and who foresee a future of possibilities, can be out of touch with a harsh reality. I'm reminded of Cornelius Eady's haunting poem in which the dying father glares at the caregiving son "with the anger that the sick have for what a healthy body cannot know." That morning in the kitchen was more than a humorous Kodak moment of delight; this was a teaching moment about aging. My dad knew something I did not yet know.

The memory lingered. As it did, my ruminations intertwined with an earlier period when it was my body that was front and center. It was also a time when my father, then younger, had difficulty talking about bodily realities. As an adolescent, I had yearned for someone to give me at least a little bit of information and insight about the mysteries of my developing, but somehow strange body. It was my emerging sexuality that was constipated, waiting for release. I didn't even have the courage to ask nor enough awareness to know what to ask as my body did things that had not happened earlier. It was not a time of glee for me. I had wanted a comfortable father to help me with my definite lack of comfort. The contrast of that earlier time and the morning were stark. I began to imagine what it would have been like had this ninety-one-year-old been around during my adolescence. Unlike my younger dad, my aging father had no reservations talking about his body and its many functions. The morning celebration of a bowel movement was just the next chapter in a long story about details that at times seemed gross, unnecessary, and endless. What amazed me was that my dad DID talk about his body with an ease that was so in contrast to the dad I had known during adolescence. And I'm confident that had I chosen that day to talk with my father about my almost sixty-year-old body, he would have listened without embarrassment or distress. In fact, he would probably have been thrilled. Where and how he learned this, I don't know. That could be another conversation.

My anger from that earlier period had passed long ago. Dad's constipation had just passed. I, too, had come to new levels of comfort with my body. We went on to breakfast, spiced with a special glee. Meal times can be memorable — this one was for sure.

"Going Down Slow" from *You Don't Miss Your Water: Poems* (1995) by Cornelius Eady. New York: Henry Holt and Company, p. 23.

Power

(My intention was to write something in which the following piece by Anna Quindlen would have appeared. My appreciation for it can be measured by my frequent use of it in workshops and sermons. It says better than most what I believe about a personal God and a personal experience of faith, especially in interactions with people of faith. After reading and re-reading her words again, I decided to let her words speak for themselves.)

At two o'clock in the morning I am awakened by the appearance of a person no taller than a fire hydrant, only his black eyes visible over the horizon of the mattress. "What do you want?" I whisper. "Nothing," he whispers back.

What can have woken my younger son and brought him down from the third floor to stand here in his blue pile Dr. Dentons? It usually boils down to some small thing: a glass of water, a night-light, a token rearrangement of the blanket. I always suspect that, if he could put it into words, the explanation would be something else entirely: reassurance that he is not alone in a black world, that nothing horrible is going to happen before daybreak, that someday he will sleep the sure, steady, deep sleep that his elder brother sleeps in the twin bed next to his own. His search for reassurance leads him to our bed, where two terribly fallible people toss and turn, the closest thing he knows to God.

This is what no one warns you about when you decide to have children. There is so much written about the cost and the changes in your way of life, but no one ever tells you that what they are going to hand you in the hospital is power, whether you want it or not.

From "Power," *Living It Out Loud* by Anna Quindlen (1988). New York: Random House, p. 136-137.

Chronic Smiling

From my mother I have inherited smiling
Chronic smiling
A non-fatal condition
Especially useful upon meeting others
Or as camouflage
When feeling down and out

On her better days
Her smile could fill the house, the room, a heart
The power of it illuminated a wide circle
A smile can be something to cherish
There are too few real smilers like my mother

Often smiles are weakened
Even altered
By negative viruses that arrive unannounced
Carried by family and friends
Spiking temperatures with sarcasm and complaints

Mom held her own when these intruders arrived
Her smile and reframing
Could soften even the hardest heart
Her smiles were more than schmaltz
She was convinced that smiles win

Now, I ponder what I have been given
Smiling, even as I muse about her gift,
Wondering how I have adapted her practices
Wondering if my children saw enough smiles
Wondering if smiles really do win

Another Time

(Uncle Arthur was one of four siblings of my mother. He and his family surrounded me with special love and care as a child. Even with the passage of time, his care lingered and surfaced again when I got the news from home that he had died. He was in North Carolina; I was in northern Britain. This reflection was written after the workshop that day.)

If we had had another time, what would we have said? Would we have reminisced, shared memories of times past that we both cherished, especially the family gatherings? Or would we have updated each other with current stories?

Could we have moved beyond the easy and the comfortable with one another to honestly talk to each other? Neither of us liked to think that this time might be the last time.

I know what I would like to have said:

I have loved you.
I have known your love for me and for my families.
I learned some things from you about gentleness,
> *About quiet dignity*
> *About genuine presence*
> *About family ties*
> *About caregiving*
> *About welcoming*
And I want to thank you for these and other gifts you have given to me.

I wish I had told him these things and more. Even though I think he knew some of these things, I regret not saying them clearly before it was too late.

When I got the news I was at a hospice in the north of Britain. I was about to start an all-day workshop with staff. So far away and yet such an appropriate place. Hospices, like the one I was in, are often tranquil, peaceful, inviting places... places like those shared with Uncle Arthur. So, before starting our work, I shared the following poem and some words about my dear uncle. Then, the work began. Somehow, the day was enriched.

Perfection Wasted

And another regrettable thing about death
is the ceasing of your own brand of magic,
which took a whole life to develop and market —
the quips, the witticisms, the slant
adjusted to a few, those loved ones nearest
the lip of the stage, their soft faces blanched
in the footlight glow, their laughter close to tears,
their tears confused with their diamond earrings,
their warm pooled breath in and out with your heartbeat,
their response and your performance twinned.
The jokes over the phone. The memories packed
in the rapid-access file. The whole act.
Who will do it again? That's it: no one;
imitators and descendants aren't the same.

There is a country music song, "The Greatest Man I Never Knew," that ends with the daughter saying that he never said he loved me: guess he thought I knew. I have often thought of those lines as too many of my friends and family have died, many abruptly. Seize the moment, say the words, don't wait until it's too late have become mantras for me. Those thoughts were there also when my Uncle Arthur died, provoking me to share the poem by John Updike with colleagues in England.

What were your reactions to my reflections, especially to the notion that we should say words of care and love sooner rather than later?

Is there a line in John Updike's poem, "Perfection Wasted," that spoke to you? What is it and what happened as you read the line?

_____

_____

_____

_____

_____

_____

_____

_____

_____

_____

_____

_____

_____

_____

_____

_____

_____

Sitting Alone

Once,
In a busy hotel restaurant,
Alone at a table,
I, not lonely,
Just alone,
With a tearful heart

Soon grief came to my table
The same grief that accompanies many
To crowded or empty places.
I should not have been surprised
Food often accompanies mourners
Tears can flavor a meal.

Grief knew me well
From previous meetings,
Times I should have remembered,
As always she looked familiar
But also different than before

The night was still young.
Grief could make for a
Welcome partner, I thought,
Especially when alone, not lonely,
If only I dared engage my guest in conversation
Or dance together the mourner's dance.

Begun after a friend's death in 2003, while traveling through the United Kingdom.

"Later"

"Later," they said, meaning, until the next time. "Later" was their way to say "So long, good-bye, farewell," except it did not contain the finality of other salutations. "Later" also conveyed a casual, laid-back dimension that I admired.

My comings and goings with my sons were, for me, emotionally charged encounters to remember, rites of passage blown out of proportion, because we were more experienced at coming and going than we were at staying. Hanging in or out with each other was not as familiar to us as some other fathers and sons. "Later," as a result, was ripe with emotion for me. "Later" always said more about stopping, when I thought we had just gotten started.

"Later" may also have been painfully pointed commentary by my sons, a paradoxically poignant message sent in my direction. When said to me, the father who had moved miles away from their first home, "later" could have meant, "Dad, it's a little late," when stay had been desired. "Later" could have been an angry statement by children of divorce.

Regret lingers. It stays longer and later than you want it to.

"Later" has often meant for men, like me, a desire to avoid the inevitable but sticky situation, about which it has long been hoped that another time, another place would provide better light and better perspective for facing, if faced at all. When such subjects are put off until later, especially a lot later, you sometimes forget what the issue was in the first place, or you hope they or you will. Could that have been a part of "later?" Were they or I putting something off which deserved attention, now, not later?

Some people put off their "later" until it's too late. I don't want that, for me or my sons. Regret lingers. It stays longer and later than you want it to.

Still, I like "later." It's not mine for the taking, of course. I'm too old to be hip or cool. More important, "later" is the language of my sons. Like cross-cultural travelers, this particular father/son challenge has been finding common words of connection, however brief, occasional, or intense. We don't need a translator to help us decipher all the possible meanings of one word nor a cartographer to tell us from where we have come or where we are going. What we need, or more to the point, what I want, are ever-increasing moments when "later" is transformed into now, an extended now.

I'm waiting. Guess that extended now will happen later.

A prose poem begun later than necessary, hopefully not too late.

Stories of estrangement or strained relationships are common in the Bible. Cain and Abel, Joseph and his brothers, and Mary and Martha come to mind. I also think of an old adage that it is impossible to NOT communicate. Silence, it is said, is one of the most powerful communication tools we possess. While my story is not a story of silence, more is said between the words than through them. What advice would you give to me or to my sons?

_____

_____

_____

_____

_____

_____

_____

_____

_____

_____

_____

_____

_____

_____

_____

_____

_____

_____

_____

_____

_____

_____

Too Many Platitudes

I went looking for hope the other day
Looking, it appears, in the wrong places.
Instead of acknowledgement of my grief
I got cheerfulness and

> optimism
>
> distance
>
> easy faith and
>
> platitudes.

Many platitudes, too many platitudes,
Which instead of comfort, raised questions,
Hard questions,
For which I have few if any answers.

I was told to look on the bright side, look for the silver lining.
Don't they know it's hard to see bright in the dark.

If all you can say is something good, the rule of many,
There are days and weeks when I will be speechless.
Tell me, tell me how is that helpful?

Tell me, will you, how do the tough get going?
For, you see, my tough did the going, not me.

Don't feel bad, you can get a new one, someone suggested.

New, I wanted to scream, is not always better and I'm not ready
    for new right now!

Someone reminded me that God does not give more than you
    can take.
Tell that to Jesus, I thought.
Remember "My God, why have you forsaken me?"
I'm with Jesus on that one.

I was told to keep my chin up
Tell me how, when my grief,
like a heavy magnet, is pulling in the opposite direction?

Look at what you do have, some said.
Try that, I say,
When there is a big hole dominating your line of vision.

Be wary, my friends, of platitudes. When someone is looking for hope,
they need more than cheerful but empty words. At least I did. I need
you more than your words.

*W*ell-intentioned desires to make things better can be offensive to grieving people who would prefer acknowledgement and empathy, not cheer-up. What do you think about that? What do you want from others when sad or sorrowful?

_____

_____

_____

_____

_____

_____

_____

_____

_____

_____

_____

_____

_____

_____

_____

_____

_____

_____

_____

_____

_____

_____

_____

Waking Up:
A Man's Breakthrough Day

It started last night. I went to sleep not knowing someone had left gum on my pillow and now there's gum in my hair and when I got out of bed this morning I tripped on my daughter's skateboard, or was it my wife's briefcase, and, by mistake, dipped my tie in the cat's water tray. I began to have a premonition that it was going to be a terrible, horrible, no good, very bad day.

After changing my tie and putting a Band-Aid on my knee, I went downstairs for my breakfast and found a note from my wife that said, "See you tonight, have a good day. I'm really looking forward to coming home to the dinner you are preparing for the family." I knew, then, it was going to be a terrible, horrible, no good, very bad day.

The kids were begging for food when all I wanted to do was read my paper and have a cup of coffee before heading off to work. When I looked where the cereal was supposed to be, all I found was Hamburger Helper and taco shells and the kids were demanding French toast. I was confident it was going to be a terrible, horrible, no good, very bad day.

When I finally got to work twenty minutes late and with just discovered egg stains on my slacks, right near my crotch, I was told by my boss of a required, immediate meeting which could be short or long — he didn't know — before which I got a call from my secretary telling me she would not be coming in because of a sick parent and court date with her former husband and when I exclaimed about all that had to be done that day, she yelled into the phone, "All you men are alike." I had no doubt that it was going to be a terrible, horrible, no good, very bad day.

Later I decided to call my tennis buddy for lunch, looking for some bright spot in an otherwise terrible, horrible, no good, very bad day only to discover that he was in a men's group that met over lunch and that he was committed to the group, especially since it had bonded, and that it was his turn to share his story and therefore he could not meet me for lunch. I thought to myself, I just want chicken gumbo and all I'm getting is mumbo jumbo about bonding and stories and sharing. This was turning out to be a terrible, horrible, no good, very bad day.

When I woke up this morning, the picture of manhood with which I went to bed was no longer to be found anywhere in my household or at work.

I knew by then that it was time to slow down. Something was going on. I thought to myself, when I went to bed last night, I knew what it meant to be a man and so slept peacefully. When I woke up this morning, the picture of manhood with which I went to bed was no longer to be found anywhere in my household or at work. Everything around me seemed in an uproar. I asked myself, "If this is not a terrible, horrible, no good, very bad day, then what is?"

I could hardly get any work done that afternoon pondering what was going on around me. In the midst of my stewing, while still trying to get the egg off my pants, I remembered that my Dad used to say, "If you're beating your head against a brick wall, you had better turn around and try another path. That one appears to be blocked." I didn't know exactly what that meant, but it sounded like I had better start over. It was abundantly clear to me that if the day kept going the way it had started, it would turn out to be the most stupendously terrible, horrible, no good, very bad day that had ever occurred.

So, that night, while we were eating the pizza I had picked up on the way home, I said to my family, "Hey, I've been having a terrible, horrible, no good, very bad day. We need to talk."

Adapted with apologies and appreciation to Judith Viorst, author of *Alexander and the Terrible, Horrible, No Good, Very Bad Day* published by Aladdin Books in 1972.

First published in *Men Talk*, summer 1990.

Changing Places

I saw it first through her eyes
That's how it often happens
The storyteller's story includes places

It was a place of pain
It was a place that reminded her of all she had lost
It was one of those places she got to know too well

It was also a place of hope
It was where she found her voice
           Writing in ways she had dreamed about
It became a community place
           She met people she would never have known
           And after knowing them
Would have regretted not meeting

She took me to this place
First through stories and poems and more stories
Then she took my hand and brought me to experience
The wonder when a place unknown, even off-putting
Becomes familiar
And when something familiar becomes home

(Written in tribute to Sue Zabel, former patient at Lombardi Cancer Center, the place described in this poem. While a patient, Sue participated in the Expressive Writing Program through which she found healing, even though curing was not possible.)

"Changing Places," a poem in *Lombardi Voices Volume III*. Washington, DC: Lombardi Cancer Center, fall 2005, p. 2.

*E*xpressive Arts Programs, like the one referred to on the previous page, use writing, literature, and other art forms to aid people in expressing something about their conditions or situations. Here is an example, a portion of a prayer:

Teach me the ways of courage past bravado,
That whether death comes gently or harshly,
Be brief in coming, or lingering,
I will be able to face it...

Teach me to be graceful in the present.

From "As even now my horizons shrink," by Ted Loder (2000) *My Heart in My Mouth: Prayers For Our Lives*. Philadelphia: Innisfree Press, Inc., pp. 153-155.

Write a line or two of a prayer you have written or might write when faced with something like cancer.

_____

_____

_____

_____

_____

_____

_____

_____

_____

_____

_____

_____

_____

_____

_____

_____

Like An Uncle

Emerging from the ice cream store, an inviting bench in sight, I knew this was the time to try and clarify our relationship. We had been talking about our "new family" as we had approached the store; so the time seemed ripe. Grasping for words to express the confusing feelings and thoughts that had been blending inside me for weeks, I blurted out my question, "Beth, when you think about me or describe me to your friends, what words do you use? What do you say?"

Typically thoughtful, my then twelve-year-old stepdaughter paused and emotionally blurted out, "I'm glad you haven't tried to replace my father. I would have gotten mad about that."

"You're right," I responded, "I know how important your dad is to you. I will never try to take his place. But if I'm not a father, what am I? Who am I to you?"

It was then that the ingenuity of children to make sense of confusion showed itself again. "Well, sometimes you're sort of like an uncle or an older brother, to which she added with a grin, a much older brother. And sometimes I think of you like an adult friend."

"Thank you," I said, "I'll take all of those as a compliment."

While the conversation continued, this part of it has lingered with me. It represents more than the growing, early relationship between two particular people, my stepdaughter and me. It is also the centuries old ritual of naming and fitting people together in relationships. While a similar ritual occurs in most relationships, it has become especially common and important in stepfamilies. Legally unattached except through the birth-parent, stepchildren and stepparents frequently seek ways to make sense of their new connections. My sons asked me shortly after my marriage to the woman who then became their stepmother, "Dad, if you died, what would we be to Marge (my wife) and Beth and Brian (my stepchildren)?" They were trying to figure out — in developmentally concrete ways — their current and future ties to the people that had been added to their lives, now also called family.

The disciples wondered about their relationship with Jesus. And Jesus, in turn, wondered what words they used to describe him.

Even though a special challenge in stepfamilies, the search and need for clarity about relationships is universal. My father wondered about his relationship with his wife of over 65 years as her memory loss deepened. Former peers wonder about their relationships after one gets a promotion and is now a supervisor. The disciples wondered about their relationship with Jesus. And Jesus, in turn, wondered what words they used to describe him. After over thirty years of sectarian violence that has pitted neighbor against neighbor, many in Northern Ireland wonder about their current and future relationships with the onset of peace. "Who are we to each other now" seems to be a common question.

I have a T-shirt on which there is a picture of a panda in the pouch of a kangaroo and the words, "I Am A Stepparent." Years after my conversation with Beth, a colleague offered me and my children a wonderful image when he said that children in stepfamilies could be some of the luckiest of children by having more than two parental adults who love and care for them. I wish I could have said something like that while my new daughter and I ate ice cream long ago. I hope my stepfamily experiences will aid me in knowing that there are many ways of connecting. Lions and lambs can lie down together. Kangaroos can carry pandas. And stepparents can be unusual but loving uncles, brothers, friends... even parents.

Adapted from an earlier version, published in *Nurturing News*, September 1985.

"*W*ho do people say that I am?" Choose some person or group that you would like to name in a different way than commonly practiced. What name would you use? Write about that new name and the wish for things to be different.

_____

_____

_____

_____

_____

_____

_____

_____

_____

_____

_____

_____

_____

_____

_____

_____

_____

_____

_____

_____

_____

_____

_____

_____

Internal Roadmaps

I traveled recently down a path
I did not recognize.
I called it transition,
            loneliness,
                    adjustment.
Strange isn't it,
How seasoned travelers,
Professional journeymen
Sometimes forget or lose their maps?
I knew grief was up ahead;
But when I got there I did not see it.
How could I miss the obvious,
Not to name my experience for what it was?
How much like grief!

Published in the *Journal of Pastoral Care*, vol. XLI, 1, March 1987.

The Crowd at the Stable: Were You There?

*T*he other night we had a party at our house. In this instance, it was a gathering of people from my place of work, colleagues and friends with whom I spend my working hours. It was in many ways your typical holiday party: plenty of food, special treats made for the occasion, jokes, laughter, carol singing, and people coming and going.

In the midst of the first round of eating, someone arrived. No big deal, you might think. Others had just appeared; still more would come later. Yet, it was different. People stopped eating. Jokes were left in mid-sentence. From several rooms the party converged on the new arrival. The cause for attention was a colleague not seen by most for more than a month and, even more so, for the three-week-old infant she held in her arms. Ian, the infant, was the center of attention for the next hour before mother and son departed.

We smiled, we cooed, we competed for holding rights. We moved our food and our conversations in the direction of this wee one. The babe was hardly aware of people or sounds, certainly not able to distinguish the rash of men and women hovering around. He added nothing directly to the conversation, neither sang or said anything memorable. Yet he, for that brief hour, was the center of attention.

...to allow yourself to become the critic or the scrooge is probably to deny yourself the experiences of wonder, grandeur, and joy that Christmas is all about.

And so it was at another time and place. Many years ago, another babe was the center of attention. We have been told that a crowd gathered to see the child. Some traveled long distances, others left animals unattended or less securely attended. No doubt others, out for an evening stroll heard or saw the commotion and wandered in, just as I and my colleagues did. Gifts were offered. It was a special time.

There is something irrational about Christmas. To ask too many questions, to think too often about the commercialism of the holiday, to allow yourself to become the critic or the scrooge is probably to deny yourself the experiences of wonder, grandeur, and joy that Christmas is all about. It was irrational for a three-week-old, non-talking, didn't-even-bring-any-food infant to take over an employee party. It was irrational for shepherds to leave their flocks. It was certainly irrational for three allegedly wise men to follow a star to see a child. It's almost impossible to get your own counselor, or doctor, or lawyer to make a house call. And these guys, these wise men, were from another county, another state, yes, even another country. Irrational!

I wanted to hold Ian at that party, to have him to myself, the others would not allow it. Ian moved from one set of arms to another, just as Jesus jumped from the disciples into the arms of Zacchaeus, and from there into the arms of the prostitute, to Peter, to Mary Magdalene... to conservatives and liberals, to Americans and to Armenians, to non-believers and Christians alike.

The crowd at the stable and the party were motley groups, a strange mix of scholars and farmers, transients and aristocrats, animals and people. Irrational! Sometimes it takes a child to bring people together and teach us some important life lessons.

This is a slightly modified version of an article that appeared in the *North American Moravian* in December 1987.

Stress Fracture

I heard today what too many fathers know in their heart of hearts but never want to hear out loud. Like a record with its needle stuck, I have been repeating over and over again the words heard just hours earlier. While I can vouch for the accuracy of the words, their meaning is no doubt tarnished with each mile I drive further from my son. I'm not sure I knew then or even know now what my son meant, really meant. Nor am I confident that he knew. It will take months or years, if it ever occurs, for us to experience simultaneous translation and mutual meaning. Technical translations aside, however, something profound was said and even a partial interpretation can be immediately understood by the heart.

My son said that we had never been close. He added that he has had trouble opening up to me and others. Somehow, it was a relief to hear about others; I wasn't the only one. When you have wanted to be there for a child and tried to be there, but hear from him "never been close," such a statement burrows quickly and deeply into the soft underside of imagined and known parental flaws.

For years my son and I have reached for each other. The barriers between us were miles between, time apart — both following a marital end and subsequent move for me to another part of the country —and our differences. He talked about our lack of common interests. I have wanted and want now for opposites to attract and for him and me to pay less attention to what is missing and more on what we have, which I think is considerable. I said that to him firmly and lovingly, but didn't push it believing that he needed to say the words he said and live with them for a while before he could let us move closer. I hope desperately that he will. I let him know of my desire to deal with whatever I had done to create and maintain walls. I voiced my yearnings for a solid relationship, not on my terms or just to meet my expectations, but rather our mutual needs and wants.

Driving further still, I talked to myself and discovered that once again I tuned most easily into my head channel — my rock and my quicksand — there hearing myself say words and phrases like, "normal development, emancipation, growing up, remember the close times he is momentarily forgetting, avoid over-reaction," even "a good fight might be good for both of us." But, try as I might, my head channel kept being drowned out by another signal, a louder signal, sent directly from a broken, no, more accurately, a cracked heart. Call it a stress fracture. Welling up from somewhere deep inside all I could hear were the desperate screams of a father looking an honest son in the face. It was so stressful I wished I was not the sole designated driver and passenger. Because I was, his words, like a stuck record, kept playing over and over again.

But, try as I might, my head channel kept being drowned out by another signal, a louder signal, sent directly from a broken, no, more accurately, a cracked heart.

I began to wonder if my son was reacting in any way similar to his old man. Might he too be replaying our interaction? Or might my tear-filled musings be little more than disappointment that a Dad's desire for a good time at his son's college turned into an unexpected sensitivity group for two, followed, of course, by the predictable and planned for request for more money? Could his announcement, accompanied as it was by affirmations of his independence, have been less a statement of yearned for and missed connections and more a recognition of differences, of two people walking their own paths? Was this another step in his growing up and out?

Whatever it meant there and then and here and now, I knew it hurt. Exegesis of parent/child dialogue is at best a risky discipline. In this case, clarity of content was not the issue. I hurt. For even if my son was saying nothing negative about his relationship with me I knew that I felt pain for what I had wanted to give to and receive from him. The stress fracture was within me.

Counselors wisely urge encounters between generations in order to clear the air, say things unsaid that need to be said, and promote healing of long festering wounds. My son and I may need such a meeting, but not now. No, in these moments I choose to open my door and let my own grief, long locked outside, in. And I tell this previously unwanted guest, "Come in, stay awhile." Tell me all you can about my life as a parent. I think there is a lot I do not know.

Begun in the summer of 1990.

It was a wise and crucial decision I made. Hindsight wise it was. I can't take credit for thinking clearly as I drove further away from my son. The credit I give myself now is that with each additional mile of distance between me and my son I came closer to myself... and, ironically, closer to my son as well. My impulse was to stop the car and call him, close the distance through words, through reaching out and back to him. My mean-spirited self wanted to blame him for being rude to his noble father who had traveled miles only to be treated so badly. My rational self, the rock and quicksand parts of me named earlier, would have been willing to rationalize even more, to conclude all kinds of imaginative reasons for my son's behavior.

But something kept me from turning fully to any of those and other options. Something told me it was time, high time, to face the pain of his disclosure. The stress fracture was mine; it was my loss of dreams.

*L*oss of dreams has become a major theme in my work and writing. Many people have told me stories about how their lives (or specific moments) have not turned out the way they had assumed or expected. "I never expected this" is a common cry in the face of cancer, infertility, conflict in congregations, mental illness, loss of job, and much more. I have come to believe, as discussed in the previous chapter, that it can be necessary to grieve shattered dreams in order to create new dreams. I was imposing MY picture of a certain relationship with my son, a picture he did not share. I had to let go of my picture and dream in order for us to build something we could both create and accept.

Reflect about expectations that have been taken, shattered, or lost for you.

Then, ponder how hope and healing can be found, even from tragedies and shattered dreams. A woman with multiple sclerosis wrote that she would not wish the condition on anyone, but that she had learned some things she never would have learned if she had not lived with MS.

I've written two booklets and many articles about shattered dreams. For more information, contact <bowma008@umn.edu>.

In the following poem, Warren Molton challenges people of faith to examine their beliefs. It was published at a time when Bible verses were too often used only to support a particular position, not for discernment or as an invitation to dialogue. It appeared when people's beliefs were questioned and when their manner of living and practicing their faith did not match the "code" required by some who acted as if they and they alone knew what was right and wrong. Like Jesus with the Pharisees of his day, Molton asserts the value of humility when affirming one's faith.

This is one of the pieces in this book that will probably provoke some type of response. A blank page follows the poem for your own thoughts.

If God is Your Answer

If God is your answer to every question,

      eternal and absolute

      once-and-for-all kind of answer,

      without a doubt,

      no wondering, dithering, or hypothesizing

      no clever juggling,

      struggling, pondering, or agonizing

      no raised eyebrow or pursed lips,

      no tilted head with faraway gaze —

just straight out, eyes glazed,

one syllable,

constant and unequivocal,

you smiling, smiling, always smiling

sweetly to every question:

God;

Then,

all questions vanish,

all questions perish,

and you stand like a post

from one of your fences,

not even enough of you

for the upright

of a cross

like one Jesus chose at the end,

facing death, and desperately

asking the ultimate question:

God, where are you?

and hearing nothing,

resigned to silence,

said, Nevertheless, I AM

and died the Lamb

still with the question.

Now there's an answer,

God.

Perhaps I Shall Sing More

*T*raveling home from a trip that included wedding plans, morning sickness, and wish lists, and meeting my future and imminent daughter-in-law and mother of my first grandchild for the first time, as well as her parents, I turned on a CD and listened to the traditional music of the Andes and Ecuador. As I listened to its vibrant energy and, to my American ears, its upbeat, positive sound, I was reminded that my Hispanic colleagues have taught me that music is often a personal, family, and community asset among Hispanic peoples. Music has helped people survive tough times and provided a vehicle for expression of their hopes and their pain. Perhaps, I shall now sing more.

Like the shoemaker and his children's shoes, the doctor and her children's ailments, I, the family educator, know too much... or too little. In either case, I know enough to be scared witless and hopeful enough to dream alongside my risk-taking son and his soon-to-be-bride. Like all parental back-seat drivers, I am yelling "slow down" all the while the accelerator is locked on fast forward. Will someone teach me to sing?

> **Like all parental back-seat drivers, I am yelling "slow down" all the while the accelerator is locked on fast forward.**

Both of these young people are adults. They can vote, sign legal documents, write their own will, and access any and all the privileges and responsibilities of all adults in this society. Not only can they, but most of these and more they have done and will continue doing. Further, I have great faith and trust in my son's ability to face and deal with life. For he has been tested more than someone his age should have been and he has been remarkably resilient. My confidence in him and my beginning impressions of his partner cause me to believe their relationship can be vital and strong. Yet, I tremble when I say these words.

Is mine the worry and anxiety of all parents as their first-born announces this particular life change? No doubt. Is my quaking knowing too much about the risks of simultaneous marriage and pregnancy? No doubt. Is my stomach churning because of a growing sense that the world they face includes pressures couples in the best of circumstances will have trouble mastering without huge costs? You bet. I have more confidence in these, my children, than I do in the possibilities for their finding jobs, adequate housing, maintaining insurance, finishing school, and arranging quality child care because of insensitive governmental and work place policies. What song can I sing to help me through my tremors? Which song can help me express my angst so that I can be there for these two, leaving my fatherly scares for other times and places?

The Memory of Pain

The memory of pain, could it be more severe than the reality?

What, then, for one with memory loss? Might each episode of pain be new, a novel experience, with no memory for comparison?

Might that explain the fear, the paranoid belief, that something or somebody is a trickster, that something or somebody connived to cause the pain?

Do we need memory to understand the mystery of pain? Is pain more or less tolerable because of memory? Which is preferable when pain is felt, memory or novelty?

I wondered about pain as I flew toward the next parental health emergency.

My guess was that pain, like some long unheard melody, lingers somewhere in our deep recesses waiting to be sung or heard again. Even with memory loss, the tune of pain is so embedded in nooks and crannies of memory, that whether named or not, it seems somehow familiar, strangely familiar, inviting us to sing along.

Hello darkness my old friend!

The Memory of Joy

The memory of joy, could it be better than the reality?

What, then, for one with memory loss? Might each episode of joy be new, a novel experience, with no memory for comparison?

Might that explain the unambiguous delight, the response of utter surprise that somebody called, somebody appeared, or that somebody brought a gift?

Do we need memory to understand the mystery of joy? Is joy richer because of memory? Which is preferable when pain is felt, memory or novelty?

I wondered about joy as I flew toward another time with my aging parents.

My guess was that joy, like some long passed episode, lies somewhere deep in our recesses waiting to be sung, released, or grabbed. Even with memory loss, the tune of joy is so embedded in nooks and crannies of memory, that whether named or not, it seems somehow familiar, strangely familiar, inviting us to sing along.

Joy, joy, joy… deep down in my heart.

A two-part essay begun as I flew to North Carolina late March 2003 to be with my aging parents.

Ponder the place of memory in your experiences of pain and of joy. Write some reflections here.

Teeter-Totters and Caring

When one is sick,
Especially when chronically ill,
The tendency is for attention and care
To be offered in one direction —

Standing over there,
Often just out of the picture,
Beyond our line of vision,
Is another.
Sometimes called caregiver,
Sometimes friend,
Often spouse.

Understandable imbalance,
Preferred role for some,
But whether offered with grace
Or resentment,
This one too deserves our care,
Sickness in families is a teeter-totter
Requiring balance and movement
Between two and more.
Otherwise one is either dropped
Or sent flying.

My friend knows how to teeter-totter.
He is, in fact, one of the best,
Sometimes digging in his feet thereby
Grounding his wife and all us riders.
Sometimes rising and falling with us
To places and possibilities never expected.
She is better because of his care.

Storm Homes:
Support When Needed

*T*he American humorist, Garrison Keillor, during a "A Prairie Home Companion" radio program monologue, used the provocative imagery of a storm home to describe the wondrous power of support. He told the story of school children from the countryside being assigned an in-town storm home to which they would go should there be a snowstorm during the school day that would prevent the buses from returning them home. In his inimitable style, Keillor described the supportive power of knowing there was someone in town ready and waiting to take care of him in an emergency. Even though he never utilized the assigned resource, the boy in the story imagined himself surrounded by caring people, just waiting to extend their hospitality to him. Hot chocolate, games, and a welcoming environment were parts of his picture of what awaited his arrival.

Whether he knew it or not, Keillor told a story of resiliency. For one of the protective factors for children or adults dealing with adversity — snowstorms, cancer, death, job loss — is social support. When someone believes there are supportive people easily accessible, the person benefits.

When someone believes there are supportive people easily accessible, the person benefits.

I've thought often of Keillor's imaginary storm home as I have listened to stories of disruptive changes in the lives of families or communities. Much more often than I expected, I have heard painful tales of who was not there at the moment when support was expected. Widows and widowers often read through the guest book registry after a funeral, noting who was not there as well as who was. Parents of children with special needs have often told me that people they thought of as friends failed to come forth when needed and wanted. Such stories have only reinforced the wisdom of the storm home as a metaphor for the social support many yearn to experience.

Years ago, I was in an auto accident that resulted in deep bruising to my left side, around the rib cage. The attending physician told me that I should anticipate stiffness and pain after sitting or lying for a long time. As we prepared for bed that evening, my oldest son, then 9 years of age, told me confidently that should I need anything during the night I should call him. While it was a lovely statement, for which I expressed keen appreciation, I also took it as a gesture only. For this was the sound-sleeping son that took considerable effort to wake in the mornings. I was dubious that his wonderful offer could occur. Then, during the night, I did awake and could hardly move. I whispered out my son's name and to my surprise and delight he was there nursing and helping me with my pain and immobility. My apartment had suddenly been transformed into a storm home. What I had been unable to imagine had in fact occurred.

Storm homes can be created, found, offered, and experienced. It's not just a story!

What would it take for your congregation to be a storm home?

In what ways is your home a storm home for your family and friends?

_____

_____

_____

_____

_____

_____

_____

_____

_____

_____

_____

_____

_____

_____

_____

_____

_____

_____

_____

_____

_____

_____

_____

_____

_____

Familiar Strangers

I can't remember stopping for hitchhikers. Why would I? I never had. Some early version of stranger danger had become an embedded part of my travel habit, now reinforced over 30 years of driving. Yet, suddenly, I had become aware that the couple riding with me around North Carolina was no longer my parents with whom I had begun the trip but, rather, a much older pair of elder persons. When and where they got in and my parents got out of the car, I don't know. Nor do I know how they and my parents kept changing places. I don't think I was hallucinating or on anything. Yet, this strange experience kept reoccurring. This had fast become one of the most remarkable trips I had ever had.

The trip started out to be a three generational rendezvous and celebration. My parents, ages 75 and 79, not driving long distances anymore, were to meet me at the Greensboro airport. Then, we were to head to Charlotte and Wilmington for visits with my two college-attending sons. As the plans were being made, all seemed eager for this reversal of roles and tradition. This was not to be an over-the-hills-and-through-the-woods trip to grandparents' house. Rather, student apartments, campus hangouts, and grandchildren's turf were to be the places for gathering. And I, the lucky parent and son, was pleased and excited about my caught-in-the-middle role.

My preparation, emotional preparation that is, centered on the moments when we would all be together. Mom's 75th birthday, my sons' 20th and 22nd, and my parents' 54th wedding anniversary provided rich occasions around which I hoped memories and stories would be spread.

And so it happened. It was, yes indeed, one of those trips to remember, but what I remember most are the drives between each stop and the people with whom I rode, not the times three generations of Bowmans were in one place at one time.

I had wanted the trip in part to have more concentrated time with my parents.

I had wanted the trip in part to have more concentrated time with my parents. Riding alone in a closed car for miles is one well-known way to achieve that wish. Even when staying in their home for several days, the separation of rooms and routines limited my ability to observe their health and vitality in ways I could in the same car or another motel room day after day. Desiring this special kind of parent-adult-child intimacy, the frequent appearance of the elder couple seemed intrusive and unsettling to my time with Mom and Dad.

Strangely familiar, these elder two, I could not push them from my car and mind. They DID remind me of Mom and Dad, but their arthritis was worse, stamina lesser, and age more obvious. Bathroom stops were more frequent. The pace from parking lot to restaurants was slower. The pain pills increased in number. My real parents, despite their almost four score years, were still youthful, active, vigorous volunteers, neighbors, friends, and hobby farmers. They just didn't drive long distances.

When I finally overcame my confusion and shock enough to engage the elder couple in conversation, I discovered that in spite of their infirmities and age they maintained a keen appreciation of life, the lives they had already lived, and those years yet to be. In fact, their values were consistent with my parents. Their ways of approaching life reminded me of Mom and Dad. I began to think to myself, "I bet this foursome would really enjoy each other, if they ever met." I regretted that I didn't ask the hitchhikers for their address and phone number. I could have had a gathering for them and Mom and Dad. They would have had a lot to share with each other.

P.S. When is it that we meet our ever-changing parents? When do we take off the masks we placed upon them? I know for me that whether the veil is completely or partially lifted, my parents still appear. They were there for my imaginary friends and me in childhood. They were there most recently with the hitchhikers and me. We have traveled a long road together.

Written in 1990 after a trip to North Carolina.

The Medium is the Message

There is a story about a child who approaches a Sphinx in the desert and is allowed one question of the wise figure. After much pondering the child asks: "Is this Universe friendly to me?"

When growing up in the Oak Grove Church in North Carolina, more years ago than I sometimes want to acknowledge, I was welcomed. I knew Oak Grove was my church, not just my parents' church. I knew with confidence that I was not a junior member who might someday achieve full status. No, I was a full-fledged important person from my earliest days there.

And how was this conveyed? One person stands out. Walt Snow was the head usher at that time. Walt Snow welcomed me. He missed me if I was absent and let me know so the following Sunday. He became my important childhood symbol that Oak Grove was a friendly place and I was an important part of it.

Was he trained? No. Was he delegated to do this by the Elders or other church boards? No. Were his interactions with me part of an intentional plan to let everyone know that Oak Grove was a children's place? I think not. And that, in hindsight, is the issue. I was lucky to be there when Walt Snow's ministry was active. I was also fortunate to be part of a congregation in which children

> **...I was not a junior member who might someday achieve full status. No, I was a full-fledged important person from my earliest days there.**

were often included in worship. Children ushered alongside adults in normal routines, not just on Youth Sunday. Children who went to church camp were expected to report to the congregation about their experiences. Camp was seen as an important activity, not just another "play" experience for children.

Church was seen as a life-long experience!

Looking back, I can point to this example as one of many that began my engagement with a local church. Occasionally when I now usher, I remember this story, smile, and look around for Walt Snow.

This is adapted from a longer article that appeared in the July/August 1991 issue of *The Moravian*.

Soften the Blow

Some get knocked down by what life brings
Others display an indomitable spirit that inspires

*T*he Alzheimer's came first
Later came the stroke
Robbing her diamonds and pearls
She lost the past
And her left side
She lost the stories she loved
And her mobility
Still she smiled
No matter what
"I love you"
"Thank you, dear"
"I'm just glad to be alive"
And affirmed us
"You're a handsome fellow"
"So good"
"Your hands feel so warm"
She loved us all
Grandchildren, nurses, friends

A smile can soften the blow
Especially so a genuine love of people
And of life

No doubt there was grief, loneliness, and fear
But those she kept in a plain brown wrapper
Not for public display
Allowing her smile to fill the room

It makes your dying harder, Mother
And easier
Our tears blend with smiles
Grief and unexpected joy overflow

Written in July 2006 after the hospitalization of my mother.

Spring Storms and Loss of Power

*F*or a five day period recently, our home was without electrical power. In comparison with the people of Grand Forks, North Dakota and St. Peter, Minnesota, where the storms directly hit, our loss was minor. No shingle was lifted, no basement flooded, no personal collections destroyed. Our home was intact; except we had no power.

The timing for loss of power could not have been better. It was late Saturday night, approximately the time we go to bed anyway. The only difference from most nights, apart from the power failure, was the light show and sounds that accompanied us into sleep. I fully expected to wake up the next morning to a return of power and so slept peacefully.

The next day, Sunday, was novelty day, a time for curious pleasure in making-do without power. We had to figure out what worked and what did not — water, gas stoves with electric starters, flashlights with out-of-date batteries for example — and we also began to gather candles and oil lamps just in case. We checked in with neighbors; went to our church in the neighborhood and experienced confirmation of adolescents and worship without electrical power; and began eating as much in the refrigerator as possible... again, just in case.

Monday came and went without power. By late Monday, certainly on Tuesday, I became increasingly aware of frustration and anger. What had started as a kind of lark with a lesson in back-to-basics or essentials was rapidly becoming a nuisance.

It is here that the story began to take a surprising twist that resulted in learnings and insights about grief and loss.

And just as I became more and more despondent, she reported, so do they, wanting news of change, some change.

Even as I was getting more frustrated, I knew and said to many that what I was experiencing was small in comparison with all those I was now reading about in the newspaper and hearing about through the battery-powered portable radio. The destruction to houses, trees, and cars on streets I drove through with some frequency over-rode any tendency to remove myself from the hurt and loss of others. Their loss was not impersonal. I knew where they lived. I could picture their streets and homes.

Yet, this awareness did little to assuage my rising frustration and inability to make good decisions in the face of my loss — a loss of electrical power. Instead of this being a time for improvisation, for accomplishing household tasks which did not require power, for visiting with friends, for going to museums or parks, for all sorts of options, I became increasingly immobilized. I kept anticipating that our house would be the next to be restored to power. Nearby neighbors and friends at some distance reported their power was back on. I was not proud of my inability to creatively act, which pushed me further into the tank of despair and sadness.

When I told this to a hospital chaplain friend of mine, she immediately saw an analogy with patients in the waiting area of the intensive care unit. She said that people often sit there, watching and waiting as other families receive news about their loved one. And just as I became more and more despondent, she reported, so do they, wanting news of change, some change.

Even here, I'm a bit uncomfortable with comparative pain and the above analogies. Still, the teaching for me was that power outages that disrupt normal routines can have an effect much greater than the lack of electricity. Studies of loss tell us one of the most difficult of losses is that which causes a breakdown in the community infrastructure. Deaths, divorces, diagnoses, loss of job, however awful they may be, most often occur in the context of an infrastructure which continues to operate. It is that infrastructure which provides the stability that is needed as we face disrupted personal routines. It is for this reason we move children back into school situations soon after a shooting or incident so there will be stability even while they deal with something tragic and awful in their midst.

When the power went off, my infrastructure broke down, especially since my business and home are at the same address. These major facets of my life were altered.

Because of this awareness, my appreciation for the peoples in nearby towns and my nearer neighbors whose homes were wrecked is all the more keen. Loss is always more than death, property, relationships, or health. For too many, the recent storms also included infrastructure losses. Now, I better understand the inability to make clear decisions in the face of such losses. I experienced what lack of power can really mean. It means more than lack of electricity. Internal power is most easily generated from a confidence that however overwhelmed you are personally, you can still count on "the essentials" of community life. It's a learning I won't forget!

Written following spring storms (1998) in Minnesota, storms that wreaked havoc on some, disruption on others.

Unexpected Detour

Sunday morning, sitting in church, my thoughts wandered. They moved easily from days past to the week ahead, from family worries and joys to the essay still to be written. Church, among its other purposes, is for musing. Some of my best thoughts have been birthed and buried in one hour.

On this morning in 1982, wandering thoughts took an unexpected detour. Half-attentive ears were filled with the news that Leonid Brezhnev's widow was grieving that day. The prayers of the people included his name and her name, Victoria Petrovna Brezhnev. The now grieving widow was among those to receive prayerful attention.

On that morning, years ago, in a strange and memorable moment, enemies became widows. The curtain opened and my walled heart softened. Grief humanizes.

Prayer was redefined. Passing the peace was no longer a mere and routine gesture. One morning, years ago, in only an hour wandering thoughts stopped wandering and began wondering. I started praying, never the same again.

Ina Hughes wrote a challenging prayer for children that moves from one stanza to another with children on different sides of "the fence." *We pray for children who spend all their allowance before Tuesday, who throw tantrums in the grocery store and pick at their food... And we pray for those whose nightmares come in the daytime, who will eat anything, who have never seen a dentist...*

See *A Prayer for Children.* (1995) by Ina Hughes. New York: William Morrow and Company, Inc.

How do you pray for those different than you? How do you pray for enemies? My experience that morning in church and of Ina Hughes' prayer is that both are much more specific than many prayers I hear in churches. They move me closer to my enemies and those I know from a distance. Write about your prayer patterns. Or better, pray now.

_____

_____

_____

_____

_____

_____

_____

_____

_____

_____

_____

_____

_____

_____

_____

_____

_____

_____

New Boots

Once, when planning for a vacation that was to include horseback riding and mountain hiking, I bought new boots. They were carefully selected to meet the needs of that particular trip and the many excursions that would follow. From the first time I put them on they seemed to know they were being worn by an outdoorsman-at-heart, in spite of my limited experience on steep inclines or in stirrups. Slowly, during the weeks preceding the trip, the boots began to mold themselves to my particular feet and ankles as I steadily broke them in. By the time we reached western Canada, the boots and I were ready for anything ahead.

You can imagine my shock, chagrin, embarrassment, and offense when, as we gathered in the stable lot to choose our horses, the instructor yelled out for all to hear, "Hey you, you with the new boots on!" — he was talking to me.

Or the reverse, how easily could he and his new bride be picked out of a crowd of couples as newlyweds?

To this day, I don't know what his clue was that I or my boots were new to horseback riding or outdoor living. Maybe he was having a bad day. Maybe most people bought new boots before traveling to the Canadian Rockies. Maybe he had to show the group he was tough by picking on someone and he just happened to choose me. Maybe I had bought boots he didn't like. Or maybe something showed, something about me and the way I wore new boots gave off some hint of the novice, the greenhorn, the rookie.

Last week, my son got married. Now, he is the rookie. I began to wonder in advance of the wedding if it was important for him to appear as if he knew what he was doing. Or the reverse, how easily could he and his new bride be picked out of a crowd of couples as newlyweds? And what if they did? Maybe, it was the wedding jitters, mine more than theirs, that caused me to hope for a balance of romantic excitement and the appearance of confident love. For some strange reason, I didn't want someone to see them and yell from across the room, "Hey, you newlyweds…"

The wish was mine. While I wanted in no way to diminish the ecstasy of these early weeks of marriage, I, the concerned parent, wanted there to be a strong start to their years together. Success breeds success; happiness and joy are contagious.

They say that after you've fallen off a horse you need to soon get back on. I was yelled at over thirty years ago for wearing new boots as I prepared to mount a horse. Now I am wearing the new boots of a father of a married son. Do the same rules apply? Tell me which horse to ride, but don't yell!

(Some poems or stories resonate, challenge, or spark continuing thoughts. All that and more happened after I read this poem by Jeffrey Johnson. I offer it for your own reading and ruminations).

Of how much more value are you than the birds? — Luke 12:24

Jeffrey Johnson Poem

If you can focus your eyes
on that bird on the bench,
the one in the charcoal suit
with the off-white shirt,
see that it's small and proper
with a formal tail tipping
and a head swiveling socially,
see how it flaps straight up
and lands on the same spot,
with bugs on its breath, see it
smooth and present there
and not a specimen,
an example, a kind or a type,
as a pet to be held or a carcass
for the alter or the market,
but as a small bird on a bench,
then you will have prayed,
and prayed well I would say,
as if you loved an ordinary
and otherwise unnoticed bird.

An untitled poem by Jeffrey Johnson, Sudbury, MA. The poem was selected as the winner of the 2006 Thomas Merton Foundation Poetry and the Sacred Contest. Included here with permission of the author.

Mentors and Villains

From kindergarten to board rooms,
    sleepovers to sleeping with,
      dreaming dreams to dreaming still more dreams,
     looking ahead to looking back,
A parade of persons has passed through my life.
With most the encounter was brief:
With others the clock struck many times over.

These people I mimic in ways indiscernible, yet so clear,
From whom I have learned in ways I hardly comprehend,
To whom I continue to respond and react,
My montage of encounters,
Flash before me.

I am who I am
Because,
In spite of,
Independent of,
In large and small measure,
These people;
My various mentors and villains.

Words/Food for Thought:
Intersections

(Earlier in this book, I included some brief quotes about the power of stories, quotes that gave me pause and/or insight about stories. In this chapter, you will find quotes about crossroads and intersections, especially ones involving the public and private, differences in values, and life and death. Read and consider how these writers are similar or different than your views of the world.)

My claim to be a theologian is not unlike my claim to be a pacifist. I think it important to claim the position even at the risk of being misunderstood. To make the claim not only begins the argument but, more importantly, creates expectations in others that help me live nonviolently. I have no faith in my ability to live that way because I know I am filled with violence. However, I hope by creating expectations in others that they will come to love me well enough to help me live according to the way of life I believe to be true. In like manner I find that others often use what I think to force me to be not just a thinker but a theologian.

From "The Testament of Friends" by Stanley Hauerwas. (2/28/90) *The Christian Century.* vol. 107, no. 7.

For decades, the people of Northern Ireland have lived with divisions: loyalist and republican, pro-British/pro-Irish, Catholic and Protestant, neighbor versus neighbor.

In that context of separation, Irish poet John Hewitt described walking into a Catholic church to see the stained glass windows. As he absorbed the ambience:

Not this my fathers' faith: their walls are bare;
their comfort's all within, if anywhere.
I had gone there a vacant hour to pass,
to see the sculpture and the glass,
but left as I had come, a protestant,
and all unconscious of my yawning want;
too much intent on what to criticise
to give the heart the room to realise
that which endures the tides of time so long
cannot be always absolutely wrong.

Hewitt, John, from "Freehold II: The Lonely Heart" found in *A Rage for Order: Poetry of the Northern Ireland Troubles*, edited by Frank Ormsby (1992) Belfast: The Blackstaff Press, pp. 85-86.

Hope, faith, love and a strong will to live offer no promise of immortality, only proof of our uniqueness as human beings and opportunity to experience full growth even under the grimmest circumstances. The clock provides only a technical measurement of how long we live. Far more real than the ticking of time is the way we open up the minutes and invest them with meaning. Death is not the ultimate tragedy in life. The ultimate tragedy is to die without discovering the possibilities of full growth. The approach of death need not be denial of that growth.

From *Head First: The Biology of Hope* (1989) by Norman Cousins. New York: E.P. Dutton, p. 25.

How did you respond to Norman Cousin's assertion: *Far more real than the ticking of time is the way we open up the minutes and invest them with meaning. Death is not the ultimate tragedy in life. The ultimate tragedy is to die without discovering the possibilities of full growth.* Write a response.

Stanley Hauerwas stated: *I hope by creating expectations in others that they will come to love me well enough to help me live according to the way of life I believe to be true.* Comment about his perspective and its implications for families, friends, and congregations.

_____

_____

_____

_____

_____

_____

_____

_____

_____

_____

_____

_____

_____

_____

_____

_____

_____

_____

_____

_____

_____

Afterword

We intersect — you, the reader, and I — one last time. Whether you have read all the pages or only a few, I offer my keen appreciation for your willingness to meet in these pages.

I close this book with a hymn verse by Curtis Beach, found in the *The New Century Hymnal*. It provides a partial summary of the previous pages.

> **Praise to the living God,**
> **Around, within, above,**
> **Beyond the grasp of human mind.**
> **But whom we know as love.**
> **In these tumultuous days,**
> **So full of hope and strife,**
> **May we bear witness to the way,**
> **O Source and Goal of life.**

About the Author

*T*ed Bowman is a father and stepfather of four and a grandfather of four. He is also a spouse, son, and brother.

Ted grew up in Winston-Salem, North Carolina, and has lived in the Twin Cities of Minneapolis/Saint Paul for the last thirty years.

Ted is an educator specializing in change and transition and the resulting grief and loss. He is also an ordained minister in the Moravian Church.

Ted expressed keen appreciation to:

> *My family who have tolerated my penchant for writing occasional pieces about our shared lives. My wife, Marge, deserves special mention as she has championed, critiqued, and enhanced the pieces in this book and other things I have written.*

> *Larry Christianson for his deep friendship and willingness to support my work and my writing.*

> *Deanna Hollenbach and the Interprovincial Board of Communication (Moravian Church in North America) for choosing this project.*

> *Writers and poets like Frederick Buechner, Andre Dubois, Wendell Berry, Jane Kenyon, Langston Hughes, and Leslie Silko who inspired me with their stories and poems. Ted also salutes the National Association for Poetry Therapy in the United States and Lapidus in the UK; both are organizations that support and promote writing and use of literary resources in healing work.*

$\mathcal{N}$otes:

_____
_____
_____
_____
_____
_____
_____
_____
_____
_____
_____
_____
_____
_____
_____
_____
_____
_____
_____
_____
_____
_____
_____
_____
_____
_____
_____
_____
_____
_____
_____

𝒩otes:

_____

_____

_____

_____

_____

_____

_____

_____

_____

_____

_____

_____

_____

_____

_____

_____

_____

_____

_____

_____

_____

_____

_____

_____

_____

_____

_____

_____